Click Models for Web Search

Synthesis Lectures on Information Concepts, Retrieval, and Services

Editor
Gary Marchionini, *University of North Carolina, Chapel Hill*

Synthesis Lectures on Information Concepts, Retrieval, and Services publishes short books on topics pertaining to information science and applications of technology to information discovery, production, distribution, and management. Potential topics include: data models, indexing theory and algorithms, classification, information architecture, information economics, privacy and identity, scholarly communication, bibliometrics and webometrics, personal information management, human information behavior, digital libraries, archives and preservation, cultural informatics, information retrieval evaluation, data fusion, relevance feedback, recommendation systems, question answering, natural language processing for retrieval, text summarization, multimedia retrieval, multilingual retrieval, and exploratory search.

Click Models for Web Search
Aleksandr Chuklin, Ilya Markov, and Maarten de Rijke
2015

Social Media and Library Services
Lorri Mon
2015

Analysis and Visualization of Citation Networks
Dangzhi Zhao and Andreas Strotmann
2015

The Taxobook: Applications, Implementation, and Integration in Search: Part 3 of a 3-Part Series
Marjorie M.K. Hlava
2014

The Taxobook: Principles and Practices of Building Taxonomies, Part 2 of a 3-Part Series
Marjorie M.K. Hlava
2014

New Concepts in Digital Reference
R. David Lankes
2009

Automated Metadata in Multimedia Information Systems: Creation, Refinement, Use in
Surrogates, and Evaluation
Michael G. Christel
2009

Click Models for Web Search

Aleksandr Chuklin, Ilya Markov, and Maarten de Rijke

ISBN: 978-3-031-01166-5   paperback
ISBN: 978-3-031-02294-4   ebook

DOI 10.1007/978-3-031-02294-4

A Publication in the Springer series
SYNTHESIS LECTURES ON INFORMATION CONCEPTS, RETRIEVAL, AND SERVICES

Lecture #43
Series Editor: Gary Marchionini, *University of North Carolina, Chapel Hill*
Series ISSN
Print 1947-945X   Electronic 1947-9468

Click Models for Web Search

Aleksandr Chuklin
University of Amsterdam and Google Switzerland

Ilya Markov
University of Amsterdam

Maarten de Rijke
University of Amsterdam

SYNTHESIS LECTURES ON INFORMATION CONCEPTS, RETRIEVAL, AND SERVICES #43

ABSTRACT

With the rapid growth of web search in recent years the problem of modeling its users has started to attract more and more attention of the information retrieval community. This has several motivations. By building a model of user behavior we are essentially developing a better understanding of a user, which ultimately helps us to deliver a better search experience. A model of user behavior can also be used as a predictive device for non-observed items such as document relevance, which makes it useful for improving search result ranking. Finally, in many situations experimenting with real users is just infeasible and hence user simulations based on accurate models play an essential role in understanding the implications of algorithmic changes to search engine results or presentation changes to the search engine result page.

In this survey we summarize advances in modeling user click behavior on a web search engine result page. We present simple click models as well as more complex models aimed at capturing non-trivial user behavior patterns on modern search engine result pages. We discuss how these models compare to each other, what challenges they have, and what ways there are to address these challenges. We also study the problem of evaluating click models and discuss the main applications of click models.

KEYWORDS

click model, web search, user modeling

Contents

Acknowledgments

We benefited from comments and feedback from many colleagues. In particular, we want to thank Alexey Borisov, Artem Grotov, Damien Lefortier, Anne Schuth, and our reviewers Yiqun Liu and Jian-Yun Nie for their valuable questions and suggestions. A special thank you to the Morgan & Claypool staff, and especially Diane Cerra, for their help in publishing the book in a very efficient manner.

The writing of this book was partially supported by grant P2T1P2_152269 of the Swiss National Science Foundation, Amsterdam Data Science, the Dutch national program COMMIT, Elsevier, the European Community's Seventh Framework Programme (FP7/2007-2013) under grant agreement nr 312827 (VOX-Pol), the ESF Research Network Program ELIAS, the HPC Fund, the Royal Dutch Academy of Sciences (KNAW) under the Elite Network Shifts project, the Microsoft Research Ph.D. program, the Netherlands eScience Center under project number 027.012.105, the Netherlands Institute for Sound and Vision, the Netherlands Organisation for Scientific Research (NWO) under project nrs 727.011.005, 612.001.116, HOR-11-10, 640.006.013, 612.066.930, CI-14-25, SH-322-15, and the Yahoo! Faculty Research and Engagement Program.

The discussions in this book as well as the choice of models and results discussed in the book are entirely based on published research, publicly available datasets and the authors' own judgements rather than on the internal practice of any organization. All content represents the opinion of the authors, which is not necessarily shared or endorsed by their respective employers and/or sponsors.

Aleksandr Chuklin, Ilya Markov, and Maarten de Rijke
June 2015

CHAPTER 1

Introduction

> All models are wrong but some are useful.
>
> George Edward Pelham Box

1.1 MOTIVATION

Many areas of science have models of events. For example, mechanics deals with solid bodies and forces applied to them. A model abstracts away many things that are not important to be able to predict the outcome of an event sufficiently accurately. When we want to predict the movements of two billiard balls after collision, we apply the laws of conservation of mechanical energy and momentum, neglecting the friction between two balls and between balls and the air. The model allows us to predict the movement without performing the experiment, which then only serves as a verification of our model. Without the model we would have to perform an experiment every time we want to predict future events, which is simply not scalable.

When it comes to research and development in web search, we perform many experiments that involve users. These experiments range from small-scale lab studies to experiments with millions of users of real web search systems. It is still common to perform experiments "blindly," e.g., by trying different colors of a web search UI and checking which colors yield more clicks and revenue [Kohavi et al., 2014]. However, we would not be able to advance as fast as we do now if we did not have some understanding of user behavior. For example, Joachims et al. [2005] show that users tend to prefer the first document to the last document on a search engine result page (SERP for short). That knowledge helps us to rank documents in a way that is most beneficial for a user. This is a part of our understanding of user behavior, a part of a user model. We first suggest hypotheses, which together form a user model, and then validate these hypotheses with real users.

Intuitively, a user model is a set of rules that allow us to simulate user behavior on a SERP in the form of a random process. For example, we know from numerous user studies that there is a so-called *position bias* effect: search engine users tend to prefer documents higher in the ranking [Guan and Cutrell, 2007, Joachims et al., 2005, Lorigo et al., 2008]. There is also *attention bias* to visually salient documents [Chen et al., 2012a, Wang et al., 2013a], *novelty bias* to previously unseen documents [Zhang et al., 2011], and many other types of bias that different models attempt to take into account by introducing random variables and dependencies between them. Since the main observed user interaction with a search system concerns clicks, the models we study are usually called *click models*. There are some recent efforts to predict mouse movements instead of clicks [Diaz et al., 2013], but our main focus is on click models.

An important motivation for developing click models is that they help in cases when we do not have real users to experiment with, or prefer not to experiment with real users for fear of hurting the user experience. Most notably, researchers in academia have limited access to user interaction data due to privacy and commercial constraints. Even companies that do have access to millions or billions of users cannot afford to run user experiments all the time and have to use some models during the development phase. This is where simulated users come to the rescue—we simulate user interactions based on a click model.

Apart from user simulations, click models are also used to improve document ranking (i.e., infer document relevance from clicks predicted by a click model), to improve evaluation metrics (e.g., model-based metrics) and to better understand users by inspecting the parameters of click models. We detail these applications in Chapter 9.

1.2   HISTORICAL NOTES

Perhaps the first work that uses the term "click model" is the paper by Craswell et al. [2008] in which the cascade model is introduced. This work also considers a number of other models that are based on a position bias hypothesis that had previously been established using eye tracking and click log analysis by Joachims et al. [2005]. Prior to the work of Craswell et al. a couple of models that we now call click models had been introduced for the sake of ranking evaluation [Dupret et al., 2007, Moffat and Zobel, 2008].

Following the publication of [Craswell et al., 2008], the UBM model has been introduced by Dupret and Piwowarski [2008], the DBN model by Chapelle and Zhang [2009], and the DCM model by Guo et al. [2009b]. Most click models that have been introduced since then are based on one of those three models.

In more recent years, quite a few improvements to the basic click models just listed have been suggested. For instance, once search engine companies began to present their search results as blocks of verticals aggregated from different sources (such as images or news items), click models for aggregated search started to receive their rightful attention [Chen et al., 2012a, Chuklin et al., 2013b, Wang et al., 2013a].

Overall, the development of click models goes hand in hand with their applications. For example, recent research work on analyzing mouse movements has been applied to improve click models in [Huang et al., 2012]. And as web search is rapidly becoming more personalized [Dou et al., 2007, Teevan et al., 2005], this is also reflected in click models; see, e.g., [Xing et al., 2013]. We believe these directions are going to be developed further, following the evolution of modern search engines.

1.3   AIMS OF THIS SURVEY

A large body of research on click models has developed, research that has improved our understanding of user behavior in web search and that has facilitated the usage of these models in various search-related tasks. Current studies use a broad range of notations and terminology, perform experiments using different and mostly proprietary datasets, and do not detail the model instantiations and parameter estimation procedures used. A general systematic view on the research area is not available. This, in turn, slows down the development and hinders the application of click models. The goal of this survey is to bring together current efforts in the area, summarize the research performed so far and give a holistic view on existing click models for web search. More specifically, the aims of this survey are the following:

1. Describe existing click models in a unified way, i.e., using common notation and terminology, so that different models can easily be related to each other.

2. Compare commonly used click models both theoretically and experimentally, outline their advantages and limitations and provide a set of recommendations on their usage.

3. Provide ready-to-use formulas and implementations of existing click models and detail parameter estimation procedures to facilitate the development of new ones.

4. Summarize current efforts on click model evaluation in terms of evaluation approaches, datasets and software packages.

5. Provide an overview of click model applications and directions for future development of click models.

Our target audience consists of researchers and developers in information retrieval who are interested in formally capturing user interactions with search engine result pages, whether for ranking purposes, to simulate user behavior in a lab setting or simply to gain deeper insights in user behavior and interaction data. The survey will be useful as an overview for anyone who is starting research work in the area as well as for practitioners seeking concrete recipes.

We presuppose some basic familiarity with statistical inference and parameter estimation techniques, including maximum-likelihood estimation (MLE) and expectation-maximization (EM); see, e.g., [Bishop, 2006, Murphy, 2013]. Familiarity with probabilistic graphical models is helpful; see, e.g., parts I and II of [Koller and Friedman, 2009] or the probabilistic graphical models course on Coursera,[1] but we explain the required concepts where they are being used for the first time.

The survey provides a map of an increasingly rich landscape of click models. By the end of this survey, our readers should be familiar with basic definitions and intuitions of what we consider to be the core models that have been introduced so far, with inference tasks for these

---

[1] https://www.coursera.org/course/pgm

models, and with uses of these models. While our presentation is necessarily formal in places, we make a serious effort to relate the models, the estimation procedures and the applications back to the core web search task and to web search data by including a fair number of examples. We hope that this supplies readers who are new to the area with effective means to begin to carry out research on click models.

1.4   ADDITIONAL MATERIAL AND WEBSITE

At `http://clickmodels.weebly.com` we make available additional material that may benefit readers of the book. This includes slides for tutorials based on the book and a list of resources (datasets, benchmarks, etc.) that may be useful to the reader interested in pursuing research on click models.

1.5   STRUCTURE

Our ideal reader would read the survey from start to finish. But the survey is structured in such a way that it should be easy to skip parts that the reader is not interested in. For example, if the plan is to use a click model package without modification, the reader may skip details of the parameter estimation process and go directly to the final formulas in Chapter 4.

We start in Chapter 2 by introducing the general terminology and notation that we will be using throughout the survey. In Chapter 3 we present the basic click models for web search and discuss their similarities and differences as well as strengths and weaknesses. Chapter 4 details the parameter estimation process—the process of estimating the values of model parameters using click data. Chapter 5 introduces evaluation techniques that are used to assess the quality of click models. Chapter 6 is a practice-oriented chapter that presents the datasets and the software packages available for click model experiments. In Chapter 7 we perform a thorough evaluation of all the popular models using a common dataset. In Chapter 8 we briefly discuss extensions of the basic click models that are aimed at handling additional aspects of user behavior and web search user interfaces. Chapter 9 is dedicated to applications of click models; in it we reiterate the most common use-cases for click models and detail a few concrete examples. We conclude with a discussion in Chapter 10.

CHAPTER 2

Terminology

In this book we consider click models for web search. Such models describe user behavior on a search engine result page (SERP). The scenario captured by existing click models is the following. A user issues a query to a search engine, based on their information need. The search engine presents the user with a SERP, which contains a number of objects, either directly related to the issued query (e.g., document snippets, ads, query suggestions, etc.) or not (e.g., pagination buttons, feedback links, etc.). A user examines the presented SERP, possibly clicks on one or more objects and then abandons the search either by issuing a new query or by stopping to interact with the SERP. The set of events between issuing a query and abandoning the search is called a *session*.[1]

Click models treat user search behavior as a sequence of observable and hidden events.[2] Each event is described with a binary random variable X, where $X = 1$ corresponds to the occurrence of the event and $X = 0$ means that the event did not happen. The main events that most click models consider are the following:

- E: a user examines an object on a SERP;

- A: a user is attracted by the object's representation;

- C: an object is clicked; and

- S: a user's information need is satisfied.

Click models define dependencies between these events and aim at estimating full or conditional probabilities of the corresponding random variables, e.g., $P(E = 1)$, $P(C = 1 \mid E = 1)$, etc. Some probabilities are treated as parameters of click models. The parameters are usually denoted with Greek letters (e.g., $P(A = 1) = \alpha$) and depend on features of a SERP and a user's query. For example, the examination probability $P(E = 1)$ may depend on the position of a document, while the attractiveness probability $P(A = 1)$ can be dependent on a query and the document's content.

Overall, a click model is unambiguously defined with the following:

- a set of events/random variables that it considers;

---

[1]Note that the session here applies only to one query, not a set of queries related to the same information need. While there are click models that are targeted at modeling multi-query behavior (e.g., [Zhang et al., 2011]), we are not going to study them here, but see Chapter 8 for further details.

[2]Observed events are sometimes referred to as *evidence*.

- a directed graph with nodes corresponding to events and edges corresponding to dependencies between events (*dependency graph*);

- conditional probabilities in the nodes of the dependency graph expressed by parameters; and

- a correspondence between the model's parameters and features of a SERP and user's query.

When working with click models, researchers often have a *click log* available to them. A click log is a log of user interactions with a search system by means of clicks together with the information about documents presented on a SERP. Different click log datasets use different formats and have different types of additional information, such as mouse movements or options selected in the search engines interface. We cover these aspects in more detail in Section 6.1. A sample from a click log, the AOL query log released in 2006, is shown in Figure 2.1; here, every line contains the following information: user id, query, query timestamp and, if there was a click, the rank of the clicked item and the URL[3] of the clicked item. If we have click log data, parameters can be *estimated* or *learned* from clicks.[4] Once we have the parameter values, a click model can be used to simulate users' actions on a SERP as a random process and predict click probabilities.

In this book we will often depict a click model as a graphical model. An example of a graphical model is given in Figure 3.1. We show random variables as circles, with gray circles corresponding to observed variables and white circles corresponding to hidden variables. Solid lines (arrows) between circles show the "direction of probabilistic dependence."

More precisely, we use the following definition by Koller and Friedman [2009]:

Definition 2.1   Bayesian Network.   A *Bayesian network* is a directed acyclic graph (DAG) whose nodes represent random variables $X_1, \ldots, X_n$ and the joint distribution of these variables can be written as

$$P(X_1, \ldots, X_n) = \prod_{i=1}^{n} P\left(X_i \mid \mathcal{P}(X_i)\right),$$

where $\mathcal{P}(X_i)$ is a set of "parents of X_i," i.e., a set of variables X' such that there is a directed edge from X' to X_i.

Notice that a click model does not have to be a Bayesian network and can be represented as a pure feature-based machine learning problem. One can refer to any machine learning textbook, (e.g., [Witten and Frank, 2005]) for the guidelines on how to do feature engineering and select the right learning method. While some advanced click models[5] discussed in Chapter 8 successfully use machine learning as part of the model, the focus of the book is on probabilistic Bayesian Network models.

---

[3]*Uniform Resource Locator*, an address of a resource in the Internet.
[4]*Estimation* is used more often in statistics, while *inference* is sometimes used in the models involving Bayesian framework. This process can also be referred to as *training* or *learning* as in machine learning studies. We use these terms interchangeably.
[5]E.g., noise-aware models by Chen et al. [2012b] or the GCM model by Zhu et al. [2010].

```
◀ | ▶ | 🗋 user-ct-test-collection-06  ⬍ |
AnonID  Query   QueryTime   ItemRank    ClickURL
76   cookingondemand.com 2006-03-01 11:51:39
76   www.quiltershome.com   2006-03-04 18:42:00
76   quiltershome.come   2006-03-04 18:45:11
76   mapquest    2006-03-05 09:18:53
76   http www.oestar.org 2006-03-11 19:20:22 1    http://www.oestar.org
76   f    2006-03-20 12:48:17
76   homedepot.com   2006-03-24 17:00:43
76   wror.com    2006-03-27 15:11:37 1    http://www.wror.com
76   yahoo.groups.com    2006-03-31 22:15:32 1    http://www.yahoo.com
76   www.stocko.com 2006-05-04 11:05:26
76   -   2006-05-25 16:52:44
1133    google grass    2006-03-01 14:16:16
1133    tuscaloosa alabama 2006-03-07 18:30:43
1133    riserealt.com   2006-03-12 19:34:10
1133    riserealty com 2006-03-12 19:34:35
1133    theteallsreal.com    2006-03-18 15:01:36
1133    theteallsreal.com    2006-03-18 15:03:03
1133    skytec.com 2006-03-23 15:34:54
1133    skytech 2006-03-23 15:36:22
1133    epartners.com   2006-03-23 17:11:10
1133    midtownvillagecondos.coml   2006-03-24 22:07:32
1133    huntsville real estate  2006-03-28 21:20:45 2    http://www.valleymls.com
1133    huntsville real estate  2006-03-28 21:20:45 2    http://www.valleymls.com
1133    averbush realty.com 2006-04-09 10:29:18
1133    skyyt.com    2006-04-18 08:47:22
1133    securty 2006-04-28 05:01:46
1133    bsfinternational.org    2006-05-03 09:43:58
1133    bsfinternational.org    2006-05-03 09:44:29 1    http://www.bsfinternational.org
1133    lawyers huntsville al    2006-05-11 22:41:06
1133    gle 2006-05-11 22:41:29
1133    -    2006-05-25 18:20:24
1133    -    2006-05-25 18:35:38
1133    -    2006-05-28 00:37:23
1708    familywatchgog.us    2006-03-01 21:19:06
1708    familywatchdog.us    2006-03-01 21:19:41
1708    familywatchdog.us    2006-03-01 21:19:44 1    http://www.familywatchdog.us
1708    loveday realty el paso 2006-03-01 21:27:31
1708    discovercard.com    2006-03-03 16:13:38 1    http://www.discovercard.com
1708    www.plasticsurey.com    2006-03-11 14:08:37
1708    www.plasticscuary.com    2006-03-11 14:09:32
1708    www.plasticsurgery.com    2006-03-11 14:10:21
1708    www.elpasomes.com    2006-03-12 16:39:42
```

Figure 2.1: A small sample of the query log released by AOL in 2006.

The notation used throughout the book is shown in Table 2.1. Here, events and the corresponding random variables are denoted with capital letters, while their values are denoted with lower-case letters. The expression $X = x$ means that the random variable X takes the value x, where $x \in \{0, 1\}$ in case of a binary variable. X_c denotes an event X being applied to a concept c. For example, $E_r = 1$ means that rank r was examined by a user, while $A_u = 0$ means that a user was not attracted by document u.

The *indicator function* $\mathcal{I}(\cdot)$ is defined as follows:

$$\mathcal{I}(expr) = \begin{cases} 1 & \text{if } expr \text{ is } true, \\ 0 & \text{otherwise.} \end{cases}$$

For example, $\mathcal{I}(S_u = 1) = 1$ if, and only if, a user is satisfied by document u, i.e., the value of the random variable S_u is 1. If a user is not satisfied by u, then $\mathcal{I}(S_u = 1) = 0$. In particular, $\mathcal{I}(X = 1) = x$ for any binary random variable X.

Table 2.1: Notation used in the book

Expression	Meaning
u	A document (documents are identified by their URLs, hence the notation).
q	A user's query.
r	The rank of a document.
c	A placeholder for any concept associated with a SERP (e.g., query-document pair, rank, etc.).
s	A user search session.
$\mathcal{S}$	A set of user search sessions.
$\mathcal{S}_c$	A set of user search sessions containing a concept c.
u_r	A document at rank r.
r_u	The rank of a document u.
N	Maximum rank (SERP size); usually equals 10.
X	An event/random variable.
x	The value of a random variable X.
X_c	An event X applied to a concept c.
x_c	The value that a random variable X takes, when applied to a concept c.
$x_c^{(s)}$	The value that a random variable X takes, when applied to concept c in a particular session s.
$\mathcal{I}(\cdot)$	An indicator function.

CHAPTER 3

Basic Click Models

In this chapter we present basic click models that capture different assumptions about searchers' interaction behavior on a web search engine result page. Later, in Chapter 8 we study more advanced models that take into account additional aspects of this behavior, additional signals from a user and/or peculiarities of a SERP.

To define a model we need to describe observed and hidden random variables, relations between the variables and how they depend on the model parameters. This together forms the content of the current chapter. Building on the material of this chapter, click models can be used to predict clicks or estimate the data likelihood provided that the parameters' values are known. For the question of parameter estimation we reserve a separate chapter, Chapter 4.

We start with a simple random click model (Section 3.1), two click-through rate models (Section 3.2) and a very basic position-based model (Section 3.3). Then we introduce the early click models, namely the cascade model (Section 3.4) by Craswell et al. [2008] and the user browsing model (Section 3.5) by Dupret and Piwowarski [2008], as well as the more recent DCM, CCM and DBN models (Sections 3.6, 3.7, 3.8) that are widely used nowadays. In Section 3.9 we provide formulas for click probabilities that are useful when using models for click prediction or simulation. We conclude the chapter by summarizing the differences and similarities between the models.

3.1 RANDOM CLICK MODEL (RCM)

The simplest click model one can think of has only one parameter and is defined as follows:

$$P(C_u = 1) = \rho. \tag{3.1}$$

That means that every document u has the same probability of being clicked and this probability is a model parameter ρ.

Once we have estimated the value of ρ, we can generate user clicks by flipping a biased coin, i.e., by running a simple Bernoulli process. As we show in Section 4.1.1, the estimation process for ρ is also very straightforward and reduces to a simple counting of clicks.

While this model is extremely simplistic, its performance can be used as a baseline when comparing to other models. In addition, the random click model (RCM) is almost guaranteed to be safe from overfitting since it has only one parameter.

3.2 CLICK-THROUGH RATE MODELS (CTR)

The next step beyond the random click model is a model that has more than a single parameter. As with many other parameters that we study later, they typically depend on the rank of a document, or on the query-document pair. That gives us two possibilities for click models based on click-through rate estimation, which we will present next.

3.2.1 RANK-BASED CTR MODEL (RCTR)

One of the quantities typically present in click log studies is click-through rates at different positions. For example, according to Joachims et al. [2005], the click-through rate (CTR) of the first document is about 0.45 while the CTR of the tenth document is well below 0.05. So the simple model that we can build from this observation is that the click probability depends on the rank of the document:

$$P(C_r = 1) = \rho_r. \tag{3.2}$$

As we will see in Section 4.1, the maximum likelihood estimation for the model parameters boils down to computing the CTR of each position on the training set, which is why this model can be called a CTR model.

RCTR can serve as a robust baseline that is more complex than RCM, yet has only a handful of parameters and hence is safe from overfitting. This model was implicitly used by Dupret and Piwowarski [2008] as a baseline for perplexity evaluation.

3.2.2 DOCUMENT-BASED CTR MODEL (DCTR)

Another option would be to estimate the click-through rates for each query-document pair:

$$P(C_u = 1) = \rho_{uq}. \tag{3.3}$$

This model was formally introduced by Craswell et al. [2008] and used as a baseline. Unlike the simple RCM or RCTR models, DCTR has one parameter for each query-document pair. As a consequence, when we fit model parameters using past observations and then apply the result to predict future clicks, DCTR is subject to overfitting more than RCM or RCTR, especially given the fact that some documents and/or queries were not previously encountered in our click log. The same holds for other models studied below.

In the next section we introduce a position-based model that unites the position (rank) bias and the document bias in a single model.

3.3 POSITION-BASED MODEL (PBM)

Many click models include a so-called *examination hypothesis*:

$$C_u = 1 \Leftrightarrow E_u = 1 \text{ and } A_u = 1, \tag{3.4}$$

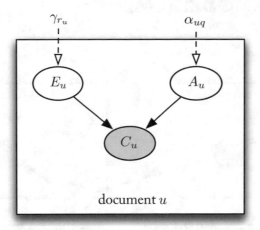

Figure 3.1: Graphical representation of the position-based model.

which means that a user clicks a document if, and only if, they examined the document and were attracted by the document. The random variables E_u and A_u are usually considered independent. The corresponding Bayesian network (Definition 2.1) is shown in Figure 3.1.

The simplest model that uses the examination hypothesis introduces a set of document-dependent parameters α that represent the *attractiveness*[1] of documents on a SERP:

$$P(A_u = 1) = \alpha_{uq}. \tag{3.5}$$

We should emphasize that attractiveness here is a characteristic of the document's snippet (sometimes referred to as document caption), and not the full text of the document. As was shown by Turpin et al. [2009], this parameter is correlated with the full-text relevance obtained from judges in a TREC-style assessment process, but there is still a substantial discrepancy between them.

Joachims et al. [2005] shows that the probability of a user examining a document depends heavily on its rank or position on a SERP and typically decreases with rank. To incorporate this intuition into a model, we introduce a set of examination parameters γ_r, one for each rank.[2] This *position-based model* (PBM) was formally introduced by Craswell et al. [2008] and can be written as follows:

$$P(C_u = 1) = P(E_u = 1) \cdot P(A_u = 1) \tag{3.6}$$
$$P(A_u = 1) = \alpha_{uq} \tag{3.7}$$
$$P(E_u = 1) = \gamma_{r_u}. \tag{3.8}$$

---

[1]It is sometimes referred to as *perceived relevance* or just *relevance* of a document.
[2]Strictly speaking, it is assumed that the first document is always examined, so γ_1 always equals 1 and we have one less parameter.

3.4   CASCADE MODEL (CM)

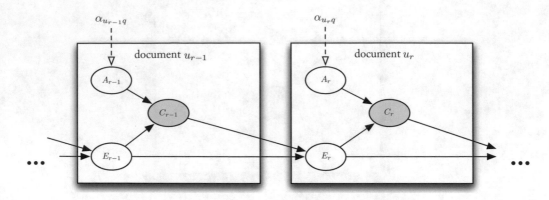

Figure 3.2: Graphical representation of the cascade model (fragment).

The *cascade model* [Craswell et al., 2008] assumes that a user scans documents on a SERP from top to bottom until they find a relevant document. Under this assumption, the top ranked document u_1 is always examined, while documents u_r at ranks $r \geq 2$ examined if, and only if, the previous document u_{r-1} was examined and not clicked. If we combine this idea with the examination assumptions (3.6) and (3.7), we obtain the cascade model as introduced by Craswell et al. [2008]:

$$C_r = 1 \Leftrightarrow E_r = 1 \text{ and } A_r = 1 \tag{3.9}$$
$$P(A_r = 1) = \alpha_{u_r q} \tag{3.10}$$
$$P(E_1 = 1) = 1 \tag{3.11}$$
$$P(E_r = 1 \mid E_{r-1} = 0) = 0 \tag{3.12}$$
$$P(E_r = 1 \mid C_{r-1} = 1) = 0 \tag{3.13}$$
$$P(E_r = 1 \mid E_{r-1} = 1, C_{r-1} = 0) = 1. \tag{3.14}$$

Note that for the sake of simplicity we use the rank r as a subscript for the random variables A, E and C and not the document u. We are going to use these notations interchangeably, writing either X_u or X_r depending on the context. The corresponding Bayesian network is shown in Figure 3.2.

This model allows simple estimation, since the examination events are observed: the model implies that all documents up to the first-clicked document were examined by a user. This also means that the cascade model can only describe sessions with one click and cannot explain non-linear examination patterns.

The key difference between the cascade model (CM) and the position-based model (PBM) is that the probability of clicking on a document u_r in PBM does not depend on the events at previous ranks $r' < r$ whereas in CM it does. In particular, CM does not allow sessions with more than one click, but such sessions are totally possible for PBM.

3.5   USER BROWSING MODEL (UBM)

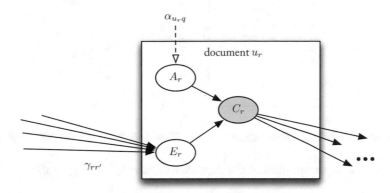

Figure 3.3: Graphical representation of the user browsing model (fragment).

The *user browsing model* (UBM) by Dupret and Piwowarski [2008] is an extension of the PBM model that has some elements of the cascade model. The idea is that the examination probability should take previous clicks into account, but should mainly be position-based: we assume that it depends not only on the rank of a document r, but also on the rank of the previously clicked document r':[3]

$$P(E_r = 1 \mid C_1 = c_1, \ldots, C_{r-1} = c_{r-1}) = \gamma_{rr'}, \tag{3.15}$$

where r' is the rank of the previously clicked document or 0 if none of them was clicked. In other words:

$$r' = \max\{k \in \{0, \ldots, r-1\} : c_k = 1\}, \tag{3.16}$$

where c_0 is set to 1 for convenience.

Alternatively, (3.15) can be written as follows:

$$P(E_r = 1 \mid \mathbf{C}_{<r}) = P(E_r = 1 \mid C_{r'} = 1, C_{r'+1} = 0, \ldots, C_{r-1} = 0) = \gamma_{rr'} \tag{3.17}$$

Figure 3.3 shows a Bayesian network for the UBM model. The set of arrows on the left means that the examination probability $P(E_r = 1)$ depends on all click events C_k at smaller ranks $k < r$. C_r, in turn, influences all examination probabilities further down the ranking (hence, the set of arrows on the right-hand side).

---

[3]Instead of the rank of the previously clicked document r', the distance $d = r - r'$ to this document was used in the original paper [Dupret and Piwowarski, 2008], which is equivalent to the form we use.

3.6   DEPENDENT CLICK MODEL (DCM)

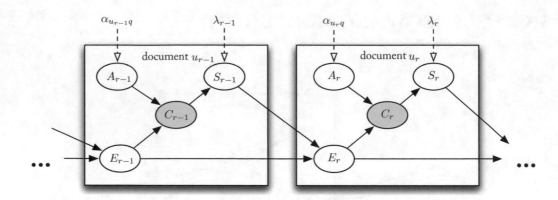

Figure 3.4: Graphical representation of the dependent click model (fragment).

The *dependent click model* (DCM) by Guo et al. [2009b] is an extension of the cascade model that is meant to handle sessions with multiple clicks. This model assumes that after a user clicked a document, they may still continue to examine other documents. In other words, (3.13) is replaced by

$$P(E_r = 1 \mid C_{r-1} = 1) = \lambda_r, \tag{3.18}$$

where λ_r is the continuation parameter, which depends on the rank r of a document.

For uniformity with models studied below and to simplify parameter estimation, we introduce a set of satisfaction random variables S_r that denote the user satisfaction after a click:

$$P(S_r = 1 \mid C_r = 0) = 0 \tag{3.19}$$
$$P(S_r = 1 \mid C_r = 1) = 1 - \lambda_r \tag{3.20}$$
$$P(E_r = 1 \mid S_{r-1} = 1) = 0 \tag{3.21}$$
$$P(E_r = 1 \mid E_{r-1} = 1, S_{r-1} = 0) = 1. \tag{3.22}$$

The corresponding Bayesian network is shown in Figure 3.4.

3.7   CLICK CHAIN MODEL (CCM)

The *click chain model* (CCM) by Guo et al. [2009a] is a further extension of the DCM model. The authors introduce a parameter to handle the situation where a user may abandon the search without clicking on a result. They also change the continuation parameter to depend not on the rank of a document, but on its relevance α_{uq}. All in all, the model can be written as follows:

$$C_r = 1 \Leftrightarrow E_r = 1 \text{ and } A_r = 1 \tag{3.23}$$

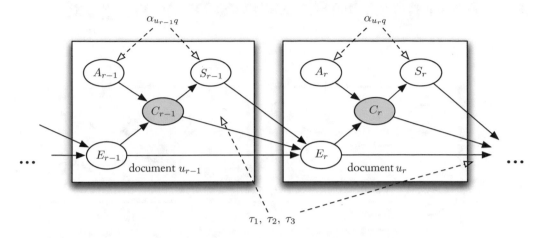

Figure 3.5: Graphical representation of the click chain model (fragment).

$$P(A_r = 1) = \alpha_{u_r q} \tag{3.24}$$
$$P(E_1 = 1) = 1 \tag{3.25}$$
$$P(E_r = 1 \mid E_{r-1} = 0) = 0 \tag{3.26}$$
$$P(E_r = 1 \mid E_{r-1} = 1, C_{r-1} = 0) = \tau_1 \tag{3.27}$$
$$P(E_r = 1 \mid C_{r-1} = 1) = \tau_2 \left(1 - \alpha_{u_{r-1} q}\right) + \tau_3 \alpha_{u_{r-1} q}, \tag{3.28}$$

where τ_1, τ_2 and τ_3 are three constants (continuation parameters).

As in the case of DCM, we introduce a satisfaction variable S_r for CCM:

$$P(S_r = 1 \mid C_r = 0) = 0 \tag{3.29}$$
$$P(S_r = 1 \mid C_r = 1) = \alpha_{u_r q} \tag{3.30}$$
$$P(E_r = 1 \mid E_{r-1} = 1, C_{r-1} = 0) = \tau_1 \tag{3.31}$$
$$P(E_r = 1 \mid C_{r-1} = 1, S_{r-1} = 0) = \tau_2 \tag{3.32}$$
$$P(E_r = 1 \mid C_{r-1} = 1, S_{r-1} = 1) = \tau_3. \tag{3.33}$$

When we write it this way, we can say that the model makes an assumption that the probability of satisfaction is the same as the probability of attractiveness ((3.24) and (3.30)). This is a rather strong assumption, since satisfaction is determined by the content of a document itself (available only after clicking), while attractiveness depends only on the document's snippet presented on a SERP.

Notice that CCM is the only model that we have considered so far that distinguishes between the continuation probability after not clicking the document (τ_1) and the continuation probability after being dissatisfied by the clicked document (τ_2). The corresponding graphical model is shown in Figure 3.5.

3.8   DYNAMIC BAYESIAN NETWORK MODEL (DBN)

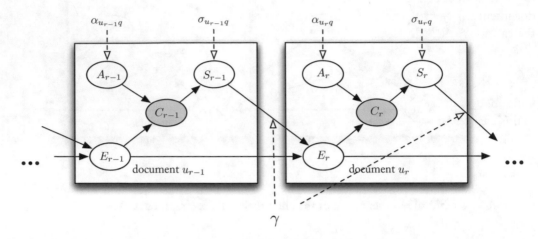

Figure 3.6: Graphical representation of the dynamic Bayesian network model (fragment).

Like CCM, the *dynamic Bayesian network* model (DBN) by Chapelle and Zhang [2009] extends the cascade model, but in a different way. Unlike CCM, DBN assumes that the user's perseverance after a click depends not on the perceived relevance α_{uq} but on the *actual relevance*[4] σ_{uq}. In other words, DBN introduces another set of document-dependent parameters. The model, then, can be written as follows:

$$C_r = 1 \Leftrightarrow E_r = 1 \text{ and } A_r = 1 \tag{3.34}$$
$$P(A_r = 1) = \alpha_{u_r q} \tag{3.35}$$
$$P(E_1 = 1) = 1 \tag{3.36}$$
$$P(E_r = 1 \mid E_{r-1} = 0) = 0 \tag{3.37}$$
$$P(S_r = 1 \mid C_r = 1) = \sigma_{u_r q} \tag{3.38}$$
$$P(E_r = 1 \mid S_{r-1} = 1) = 0 \tag{3.39}$$
$$P(E_r = 1 \mid E_{r-1} = 1, S_{r-1} = 0) = \gamma, \tag{3.40}$$

where γ is the continuation probability for a user that either did not click on a document or clicked but was not satisfied by it. The graphical model is shown in Figure 3.6.

3.8.1   SIMPLIFIED DBN MODEL (SDBN)

One special case of the DBN model is the so-called *simplified DBN model* (SDBN) [Chapelle and Zhang, 2009, Section 5] which assumes that $\gamma = 1$. This model allows for simple parameter

---

[4]This parameter is often referred to as the *satisfaction probability*.

estimation (Section 4.1.3) while maintaining a similar level of predictive power as DBN according to Chapelle and Zhang.

It is worth noting that if we further assume that a user is always satisfied by a clicked document ($S_r \equiv C_r$), in other words, if all σ_{uq} are equal to 1, then the SDBN model reduces to the cascade model (Section 3.4).

3.9 CLICK PROBABILITIES

Click models aim at modeling user clicks on a SERP. In particular, the basic click models discussed in this chapter are able to calculate the probability of a click on a given document u, i.e., $P(C_u = 1)$, and the probability of a click on that document given previously observed clicks in the same session, i.e., $P(C_u = 1 \mid \mathbf{C}_{<r_u})$.[5] The former is used to estimate the click-through rate (CTR) of a document, while the latter is useful when simulating clicks in a session one by one or computing the likelihood.

For simple click models such as RCM, RCTR, DCTR and PBM, the probability of examining a document does not depend on clicks above this document ($\mathbf{C}_{<r_u}$). Therefore, for these models $P(C_u = 1 \mid \mathbf{C}_{<r_u}) = P(C_u = 1)$. For the RCM, RCTR and DCTR models, these probabilities are directly equal to the model parameters: ρ, ρ_{r_u} and ρ_{uq} respectively. For the PBM model, the probability of a click is decomposed into the examination and attractiveness probabilities and, thus,

$$P(C_u = 1) = P(A_u = 1) \cdot P(E_{r_u} = 1) = \alpha_{uq} \gamma_{r_u}. \tag{3.41}$$

For the other basic click models, examination of a document depends on clicks above the document ($\mathbf{C}_{<r_u}$) and, thus, the full and conditional probabilities of click are calculated differently. For the CM, DCM, CCM, DBN and SDBN models, the full probability of click, $P(C_u = 1)$, is calculated as follows:

$$P(C_u = 1) = P(C_u = 1 \mid E_{r_u} = 1) \cdot P(E_{r_u} = 1) = \alpha_{uq} \epsilon_{r_u}. \tag{3.42}$$

The difference between the models lies in the way they compute the examination probability $P(E_{r_u} = 1) = \epsilon_{r_u}$. The general rule for all models mentioned above is the following (here, we use r instead of r_u for simplicity):

$$
\begin{aligned}
\epsilon_{r+1} &= P(E_{r+1} = 1) \\
&= P(E_r = 1) \cdot P(E_{r+1} = 1 \mid E_r = 1) \\
&= P(E_r = 1) \cdot \big(P(E_{r+1} = 1 \mid E_r = 1, C_r = 1) \cdot P(C_r = 1 \mid E_r = 1) + \\
&\qquad P(E_{r+1} = 1 \mid E_r = 1, C_r = 0) \cdot P(C_r = 0 \mid E_r = 1) \big).
\end{aligned}
\tag{3.43}
$$

[5]Here, $\mathbf{C}_{<r_u}$ denotes the set of observed clicks above rank r_u.

The examination probability of each model can be calculated using this equation. For example, for the DBN model it gives the following formula for the examination probability:

$$\epsilon_{r+1} = \epsilon_r \left((1 - \sigma_{uq}) \gamma \alpha_{uq} + \gamma (1 - \alpha_{uq}) \right). \tag{3.44}$$

The conditional probability of a click for the CM, DCM, CCM, DBN and SDBN models can be calculated in a similar way:

$$P(C_u = 1 \mid \mathbf{C}_{<r_u}) = P(C_u = 1 \mid E_{r_u} = 1, \mathbf{C}_{<r_u}) \cdot P(E_{r_u} = 1 \mid \mathbf{C}_{<r_u}) = \alpha_{uq} \epsilon_{r_u}, \tag{3.45}$$

where the examination probability $P(E_{r_u} = 1 \mid \mathbf{C}_{<r_u}) = \epsilon_{r_u}$ should now be calculated based on clicks observed above the document u (again, we use r instead of r_u):

$$\begin{aligned}
\epsilon_{r+1} &= P(E_{r+1} = 1 \mid \mathbf{C}_{<r+1}) \\
&= P(E_{r+1} = 1 \mid E_r = 1, \mathbf{C}_{<r+1}) \cdot P(E_r = 1 \mid \mathbf{C}_{<r+1}) \\
&= P(E_{r+1} = 1 \mid E_r = 1, C_r = 1) \cdot P(E_r = 1 \mid C_r = 1, \mathbf{C}_{<r}) \cdot c_r^{(s)} + \\
&\quad P(E_{r+1} = 1 \mid E_r = 1, C_r = 0) \cdot P(E_r = 1 \mid C_r = 0, \mathbf{C}_{<r}) \cdot (1 - c_r^{(s)}).
\end{aligned} \tag{3.46}$$

Here, we split the conditional examination probability into two parts based on the click $c_r^{(s)}$ observed at rank r in a particular query session s. All basic click models assume that a clicked document is examined, thus, $P(E_r = 1 \mid C_r = 1, \mathbf{C}_{<r}) = 1$. On the other hand, if a document is not clicked, then we cannot directly infer whether it is examined or not. Therefore, $P(E_r = 1 \mid C_r = 0, \mathbf{C}_{<r})$ should be calculated as follows:

$$\begin{aligned}
P(E_r = 1 \mid C_r = 0, \mathbf{C}_{<r}) &= \frac{P(E_r = 1, C_r = 0 \mid \mathbf{C}_{<r})}{P(C_r = 0 \mid \mathbf{C}_{<r})} \\
&= \frac{P(C_r = 0 \mid E_r = 1, \mathbf{C}_{<r}) \cdot P(E_r = 1 \mid \mathbf{C}_{<r})}{P(C_r = 0 \mid \mathbf{C}_{<r})} \\
&= \frac{\epsilon_r (1 - \alpha_{u_r q})}{1 - \alpha_{u_r q} \epsilon_r}.
\end{aligned} \tag{3.47}$$

So the final formula for the conditional examination probability is the following:

$$\begin{aligned}
\epsilon_{r+1} &= P(E_{r+1} = 1 \mid E_r = 1, C_r = 1) \cdot c_r^{(s)} + \\
&\quad P(E_{r+1} = 1 \mid E_r = 1, C_r = 0) \cdot \frac{\epsilon_r (1 - \alpha_{u_r q})}{1 - \alpha_{u_r q} \epsilon_r} (1 - c_r^{(s)}).
\end{aligned} \tag{3.48}$$

The conditional examination probability for each click model can be calculated using this equation. For example, for the DCM model this probability can be computed as follows:

$$\epsilon_{r+1} = \lambda_r c_r^{(s)} + \frac{(1 - \alpha_{u_r q}) \epsilon_r}{1 - \alpha_{u_r q} \epsilon_r} (1 - c_r^{(s)}). \tag{3.49}$$

Finally, the UBM click model has a different procedure of calculating the full and conditional click probabilities. The UBM conditional probability of click is computed as follows:

$$P(C_u = 1 \mid \mathbf{C}_{<r_u}) = \alpha_{uq} \gamma_{r_u r'_u}, \tag{3.50}$$

where r'_u is the rank of the last clicked document above u.

To calculate the full click probability $P(C_u = 1)$, we should marginalize over all possible clicks above the document u [Chuklin et al., 2013c]:

$$P(C_u = 1) = \sum_{j=0}^{r_u-1} P(C_j = 1, C_{j+1} = 0, \dots, C_{r_u-1} = 0, C_{r_u} = 1). \tag{3.51}$$

By applying Bayes' rule we can rewrite this equation as follows:

$$P(C_u = 1) = \sum_{j=0}^{r_u-1} P(C_j = 1) \cdot \left(\prod_{k=j+1}^{r_u-1} P(C_k = 0 \mid C_j = 1, C_{j+1} = 0, \dots, C_{k-1} = 0) \right) \cdot$$

$$P(C_{r_u} = 1 \mid C_j = 1, C_{j+1} = 0, \dots, C_{r_u-1} = 0)$$

$$= \sum_{j=0}^{r_u-1} P(C_j = 1) \cdot \left(\prod_{k=j+1}^{r_u-1} (1 - \alpha_{u_k q} \gamma_{kj}) \right) \cdot \alpha_{uq} \gamma_{r_u j}, \tag{3.52}$$

where $P(C_0 = 1) = 1$.

The full and conditional click probabilities for all models presented in this chapter are summarized in Table 3.1.

3.10 SUMMARY

As has become apparent from the model equations and Bayesian network graphical models, there are many similarities between the models that we have presented. In particular, all models introduce an attractiveness variable A_u and most of the models define a satisfaction variable S_u. The models then define how the examination probability E_u depends on the examination, satisfaction and click events for previous documents: $\mathbf{E}_{<r_u}, \mathbf{S}_{<r_u}, \mathbf{C}_{<r_u}$.

We summarize the parameters corresponding to these events in Table 3.2. The table shows that RCM and RCTR use a constant value for attractiveness, while the other models use a set of query-document dependent parameters α_{uq}. Satisfaction is not defined for RCM, RCTR, DCTR, PBM and UBM; it is constant for CM (satisfaction is equivalent to a click for the cascade model); it depends on the document rank for DCM and on the query-document pair for CCM and DBN. CCM and DBN use different parameters for satisfaction: CCM re-uses the attractiveness parameters, while DBN introduces a new set of parameters σ_{uq}. The examination

Table 3.1: Full and conditional probabilities of click for basic click models

Click model	$P(C_u = 1)$	$P(C_u = 1 \mid C_{<r_u})$
RCM	ρ	ρ
RCTR	ρ_{r_u}	ρ_{r_u}
DCTR	ρ_{uq}	ρ_{uq}
PBM	$\alpha_{uq}\gamma_{r_u}$	$\alpha_{uq}\gamma_{r_u}$
CM	$\alpha_{uq}\epsilon_{r_u}$, where $\epsilon_{r+1} = \epsilon_r(1-\alpha_{u_rq})$	$\alpha_{uq}\epsilon_{r_u}$, where $\epsilon_r = \begin{cases} 1 & \text{if no clicks before } r \\ 0 & \text{otherwise} \end{cases}$
UBM	$\sum_{j=0}^{r_u-1} P(C_j = 1)\left(\prod_{k=j+1}^{r_u-1}(1-\alpha_{u_kq}\gamma_{kj})\right)\alpha_{uq}\gamma_{r_uj}$, where $P(C_0 = 1) = 1$	$\alpha_{uq}\gamma_{rr'}$
DCM	$\alpha_{uq}\epsilon_{r_u}$, where $\epsilon_{r+1} = \epsilon_r\left(\alpha_{u_rq}\lambda_{r_u} + (1-\alpha_{u_rq})\right)$	$\alpha_{uq}\epsilon_{r_u}$, where $\epsilon_{r+1} = c_r^{(s)}\lambda_r + \left(1 - c_r^{(s)}\right)\frac{(1-\alpha_{u_rq})\epsilon_r}{1-\alpha_{u_rq}\epsilon_r}$
CCM	$\alpha_{uq}\epsilon_{r_u}$, where $\epsilon_{r+1} = \epsilon_r\left(\alpha_{u_rq}((1-\alpha_{u_rq})\tau_2 + \alpha_{u_rq}\tau_3) + (1-\alpha_{u_rq})\tau_1\right)$	$\alpha_{uq}\epsilon_{r_u}$, where $\epsilon_{r+1} = c_r^{(s)}((1 - \alpha_{u_rq})\tau_2 + \alpha_{u_rq}\tau_3) + \left(1 - c_r^{(s)}\right)\frac{(1-\alpha_{u_rq})\epsilon_r\tau_1}{1-\alpha_{u_rq}\epsilon_r}$
DBN	$\alpha_{uq}\epsilon_{r_u}$, where $\epsilon_{r+1} = \epsilon_r\gamma(\alpha_{u_rq}(1 - \sigma_{u_rq}) + (1 - \alpha_{u_rq}))$	$\alpha_{uq}\epsilon_{r_u}$, where $\epsilon_{r+1} = c_r^{(s)}\gamma(1 - \sigma_{u_rq}) + \left(1 - c_r^{(s)}\right)\frac{(1-\alpha_{u_rq})\epsilon_r\gamma}{1-\alpha_{u_rq}\epsilon_r}$
SDBN	Same as DBN with $\gamma = 1$	Same as DBN with $\gamma = 1$

Table 3.2: Core assumptions of the basic click models. Here, $P(A_u = 1)$ is the probability that document u is attractive, $P(S_u = 1 \mid C_u = 1)$ is the probability that a user is satisfied with document u after clicking on it and $P(E_u = 1 \mid \mathbf{E}_{<r_u}, \mathbf{S}_{<r_u}, \mathbf{C}_{<r_u})$ is the probability of examining document u based on examination, satisfaction and click events for previous documents.

Click model	$P(A_u = 1)$	$P(S_u = 1 \mid C_u = 1)$	$P(E_u = 1 \mid \mathbf{E}_{<r_u}, \mathbf{S}_{<r_u}, \mathbf{C}_{<r_u})$
RCM	constant (ρ)	N/A	constant (1)
RCTR	constant (1)	N/A	rank (ρ_r)
DCTR	query-document (ρ_{uq})	N/A	constant (1)
PBM	query-document (α_{uq})	N/A	rank (γ_r)
CM	query-document (α_{uq})	constant (1)	constant $(1$ or $0)$
UBM	query-document (α_{uq})	N/A	other $(\gamma_{rr'})$
DCM	query-document (α_{uq})	rank $(1 - \lambda_r)$	constant $(1$ or $0)$
CCM	query-document (α_{uq})	query-document (α_{uq})	constant (τ_1, τ_2, τ_3)
DBN	query-document (α_{uq})	query-document (σ_{uq})	constant (γ)
SDBN	query-document (α_{uq})	query-document (σ_{uq})	constant $(1$ or $0)$

probability is always 1 for RCM and DCTR, and depends only on the document rank for RCTR and PBM. It has a non-trivial dependency on previous clicks in UBM, while in CM, DCM, CCM and DBN it depends on the click, satisfaction and examination events at rank $(r - 1)$ and is governed by a set of constants (different for different models).

An interesting observation, which becomes evident by inspecting Table 3.2, concerns the difference between the SDBN (Section 3.8.1) and DCM (Section 3.6) models. These two models appear to be the same apart from the definition of the satisfaction probability $P(S_u = 1 \mid C_u = 1)$: for SDBM it depends on the query-document pair, while for DCM it depends on the document rank.

In the next chapter we are going to discuss the process of estimating click model parameters, which completes the picture we have begun to sketch in this chapter. Chapter 5 describes different ways to evaluate click models and Chapter 6 presents datasets and software packages useful for experimenting with click models. After reading these chapters the reader should be able to experiment with click models, modify them and evaluate them. We present our own experiments in Chapter 7.

Alternatively, the reader may now proceed directly to Chapter 8 where various advanced click models are described or to Chapter 9 where we discuss applications of click models.

CHAPTER 4

Parameter Estimation

In Chapter 3 we introduced basic click models for web search. To evaluate the quality of these models (in Chapter 5) and to use them in applications (in Chapter 9), click models first need to be trained. In this chapter we describe the process of learning click model parameters from past click observations. This process is called parameter *estimation* or parameter *learning*. We will review two main techniques used to estimate the parameters of click models, namely maximum likelihood estimation (MLE) and the expectation-maximization algorithm (EM). We will then show how each technique can be applied to parameter estimation. Several detailed examples of these techniques will be given to support the theory. Additionally, we discuss a few alternative methods of parameter estimation, but our main focus is on the MLE and EM algorithms.

The MLE estimates and EM update rules for the parameters of the click models introduced so far will be presented in Section 4.3. Readers interested in implementing those click models without modification may skip the calculations of this chapter and directly use the formulas that are summarized in Table 4.1.

The click models that we have introduced so far can be divided into two classes based on the nature of their random variables. These classes determine the way the model parameters are estimated. Click models of the first class operate with observed random variables. For example, in the simplified DBN model [Chapelle and Zhang, 2009] both the attractiveness A and satisfaction S depend on the examination event E, which is observed. In this case, maximum likelihood estimation can be used to estimate their probabilities. Click models of the second class have one or more hidden variables, the values of which are not observed. In this case we suggest to use the expectation-maximization algorithm. Below we discuss each of the two cases in detail.

4.1 THE MLE ALGORITHM

Click models consider binary events (e.g., a document is either examined by a user or not) and assume that the corresponding random variables are distributed according to a Bernoulli distribution: $X \sim Bernoulli(\theta)$, where θ is a parameter of the distribution. The parameter θ is unknown and needs to be estimated based on the values of X. In case X is observed, θ can be derived in closed form using maximum likelihood estimation. If X is not observed, the expectation-maximization algorithm should be used instead (see Section 4.2).

Given a concept c, assume that we observe a set of user sessions $\mathcal{S}_c$ containing this concept at least once as well as the values of X for all or some occurrences of c. Since X_c is a binary random variable, its value x_c can be either 0 or 1. The likelihood for the parameter θ_c can be written as follows:[1]

$$\mathcal{L}(\theta_c) = \prod_{s \in \mathcal{S}_c} \prod_{c_i \in s_c} \theta_c^{x_{c_i}^{(s)}} (1 - \theta_c)^{1 - x_{c_i}^{(s)}}, \tag{4.1}$$

where s_c is the set of occurrences of the concept c in the session s and $x_{c_i}^{(s)}$ is the value of the random variable X when applied to the i-th occurrence of c.

By taking the log of (4.1), calculating its derivative and equating it to zero, we get the MLE estimation of the parameter θ_c. In our case, this is simply the sample mean of X_c:

$$\theta_c = \frac{\sum_{s \in \mathcal{S}_c} \sum_{c_i \in s_c} \mathcal{I}(X_{c_i}^{(s)} = 1)}{\sum_{s \in \mathcal{S}_c} |s_c|} = \frac{\sum_{s \in \mathcal{S}_c} \sum_{c_i \in s_c} x_{c_i}^{(s)}}{\sum_{s \in \mathcal{S}_c} |s_c|}, \tag{4.2}$$

where $|s_c|$ is the size of the set s_c.

Below, we present several examples of parameter estimation using MLE. In particular, we focus on the RCM, CTR, DCM and SDBN click models.

4.1.1   MLE FOR THE RCM AND CTR MODELS

The simplest click model, RCM, discussed in Section 3.1, has only one parameter ρ, which models the probability of a click. The click event is always observed, so ρ can be estimated using MLE. In the case of RCM, the concept c is just "any document," so in (4.2) we should consider all sessions in $\mathcal{S}$ and all documents in each session:

$$\rho = \frac{\sum_{s \in \mathcal{S}} \sum_{u \in s} c_u^{(s)}}{\sum_{s \in \mathcal{S}} |s|}. \tag{4.3}$$

Similar to this formula we can obtain the estimation of the RCTR model (Section 3.2.1):

$$\rho_r = \frac{\sum_{s \in \mathcal{S}} c_r^{(s)}}{|\mathcal{S}|}, \tag{4.4}$$

and the DCTR model (Section 3.2.2):

$$\rho_{uq} = \frac{\sum_{s \in \mathcal{S}_{uq}} c_u^{(s)}}{|\mathcal{S}_{uq}|}, \tag{4.5}$$

where $\mathcal{S}_{uq}$ is the set of sessions initiated by the query q and containing the document u.

4.1.2   MLE FOR DCM

The DCM click model, introduced in Section 3.6, has two sets of parameters: the perceived relevance α_{uq} of all query-document pairs and the continuation probabilities λ_r for all ranks r.

---

[1]Here, we assume the simplest case where the full likelihood function can be represented as a product of likelihood functions for each model parameter.

The corresponding random variables are the attractiveness A and the opposite of satisfaction, i.e., $1 - S$. In the general DCM model, the attractiveness A is not observable starting from the rank of the last-clicked document (denoted as l here): we do not know if a user stopped examining documents because they were satisfied by the last-clicked document, or because they were not attracted by any document below it. However, if a user is assumed to be satisfied by the last-clicked document, then A and S do become observable. We will call this modification *simplified DCM*, or SDCM for short. According to the simplified DCM model, for $r \leq l$ a document u_r is attractive whenever it is clicked:

$$A_{u_r} = 1 \iff C_{u_r} = 1. \tag{4.6}$$

Also, a user is satisfied by a document at rank r whenever u_r is clicked and this is the last click in a session:

$$S_r = 1 \iff C_{u_r} = 1 \;\&\; r = l. \tag{4.7}$$

Since all random variables of SDCM are observed, its parameters can be estimated using MLE.

The attractiveness α_{uq} of a given query-document pair is defined for sessions that have been initiated by the query q and contain the document u above or at the last-clicked rank. More formally, let us consider the query-document pair uq as a concept and define $\mathcal{S}_{uq} = \{s_q : u \in s_q, r_u \leq l\}$, where s_q is the session initiated by q. Notice that the concept uq appears at most once in each session. Thus, according to (4.2), the attractiveness parameter α_{uq} of the simplified DCM model is estimated as follows:

$$\begin{aligned}
\alpha_{uq} &= \frac{\sum_{s \in \mathcal{S}_{uq}} \mathcal{I}(A_u^{(s)} = 1)}{\sum_{s \in \mathcal{S}_{uq}} 1} \\
&= \frac{1}{|\mathcal{S}_{uq}|} \sum_{s \in \mathcal{S}_{uq}} \mathcal{I}(A_u^{(s)} = 1) \\
&= \frac{1}{|\mathcal{S}_{uq}|} \sum_{s \in \mathcal{S}_{uq}} \mathcal{I}(C_u^{(s)} = 1) = \frac{1}{|\mathcal{S}_{uq}|} \sum_{s \in \mathcal{S}_{uq}} c_u^{(s)}.
\end{aligned} \tag{4.8}$$

This equation means that the attractiveness of a document is directly proportional to the number of times it is clicked and inversely proportional to the number of times it is presented for a given query above or at the last-clicked rank.

The continuation probability λ_r is the opposite of the satisfaction probability: $\lambda_r = 1 - \sigma_r$. The satisfaction event S_r, in turn, is defined for sessions, where a click at rank r is observed: $S_r = \{s : c_{u_r}^{(s)} = 1\}$.[2] Combining the above observations with (4.2), we obtain the MLE estimate of the continuation probability λ_r:

$$\lambda_r = 1 - \frac{\sum_{s \in \mathcal{S}_r} \mathcal{I}(S_{u_r}^{(s)} = 1)}{\sum_{s \in \mathcal{S}_r} 1}$$

---

[2]Sessions without clicks were excluded in the original paper [Guo et al., 2009b].

$$= 1 - \frac{1}{|\mathcal{S}_r|} \sum_{s \in \mathcal{S}_r} \mathcal{I}(S_{u_r}^{(s)} = 1)$$

$$= 1 - \frac{1}{|\mathcal{S}_r|} \sum_{s \in \mathcal{S}_r} \mathcal{I}(r_u^{(s)} = l)$$

$$= \frac{1}{|\mathcal{S}_r|} \sum_{s \in \mathcal{S}_r} \mathcal{I}(r_u^{(s)} \neq l) \tag{4.9}$$

Again, notice that the rank r that we consider appears only once in each session, so we do not need two summations in the numerator.

Equation 4.9 shows that the satisfaction probability at a given rank r is equal to the number of times r is the rank of the last-clicked document, divided by the number of times a click at rank r is observed. The continuation probability, in turn, is one minus this quantity.

Notice that the parameters of the general DCM model should be estimated using the EM algorithm because it has hidden variables. However, the paper in which DCM was originally introduced uses the same equations (4.8) and (4.9), although derived in a different way [Guo et al., 2009b].

4.1.3   MLE FOR SDBN

Similarly to the simplified DCM click model, SDBN assumes that a user examines all documents until the last-clicked one and then abandons the search (Section 3.8.1). In this case, both the attractiveness A and satisfaction S of SDBN are observed. Therefore, MLE can be used to estimate the model parameters: attractiveness probabilities α_{uq} and satisfaction probabilities σ_{uq}.

In the case of SDBN, both attractiveness and satisfaction are defined for a query-document pair. Therefore, in order to estimate α_{uq} and σ_{uq} for a given pair, we should consider sessions initiated by the query q and containing the document u above or at the last-clicked rank l: $\mathcal{S}_{uq} = \{s_q : u \in s_q, r_u \leq l\}$. Then, according to (4.2), the attractiveness probability α_{uq} can be estimated using MLE as follows:

$$\alpha_{uq} = \frac{\sum_{s \in \mathcal{S}_{uq}} \mathcal{I}(A_u^{(s)} = 1)}{\sum_{s \in \mathcal{S}_{uq}} 1}$$

$$= \frac{1}{|\mathcal{S}_{uq}|} \sum_{s \in \mathcal{S}_{uq}} \mathcal{I}(A_u^{(s)} = 1)$$

$$= \frac{1}{|\mathcal{S}_{uq}|} \sum_{s \in \mathcal{S}_{uq}} \mathcal{I}(C_u^{(s)} = 1) = \frac{1}{|\mathcal{S}_{uq}|} \sum_{s \in \mathcal{S}_{uq}} c_u^{(s)} \tag{4.10}$$

This means that the attractiveness of a document, given a query, is directly proportional to the number of times this document is clicked and inversely proportional to the number of times it is presented in response to the given query above or at the last-clicked rank.

The satisfaction event S_u is defined only for the part of the session set $\mathcal{S}_{uq}$ where a click on u is observed: $\mathcal{S}'_{uq} = \{s : s \in \mathcal{S}_{uq}, c_u^{(s)} = 1\}$. Based on this session set, the satisfaction probability σ_{uq} is estimated as follows:

$$
\begin{aligned}
\sigma_{uq} &= \frac{\sum_{s \in \mathcal{S}'_{uq}} \mathcal{I}(S_u^{(s)} = 1)}{\sum_{s \in \mathcal{S}'_{uq}} 1} \\
&= \frac{1}{|\mathcal{S}'_{uq}|} \sum_{s \in \mathcal{S}'_{uq}} \mathcal{I}(S_u^{(s)} = 1) \\
&= \frac{1}{|\mathcal{S}'_{uq}|} \sum_{s \in \mathcal{S}'_{uq}} \mathcal{I}(C_u^{(s)} = 1, r_u^{(s)} = l) \\
&= \frac{1}{|\mathcal{S}'_{uq}|} \sum_{s \in \mathcal{S}'_{uq}} \mathcal{I}(r_u^{(s)} = l).
\end{aligned}
\tag{4.11}
$$

Thus, the satisfaction probability of a document u, given a query q, is equal to the number of times u appears as the last-clicked document, divided by the number of times it is clicked for the query q.

In contrast to SDBN, the full DBN click model, discussed in Section 3.8, has an additional parameter γ. It determines whether a user continues examining documents after they are not satisfied with the current one. In this case, the attractiveness A and satisfaction S are not observable after the last-clicked document, so the EM algorithm should be used to estimate the parameters of DBN. We discuss the EM estimation method in the next section and apply it to DBN in Section 4.2.4.

4.2   THE EM ALGORITHM

Consider a random variable X and a set of its parents $\mathcal{P}(X)$ in a Bayesian network.[3] Assume further that there is an assignment $\mathcal{P}(X) = \mathbf{p}$ of the parents, such that the probability $P(X \mid \mathcal{P}(X) = \mathbf{p})$ is a Bernoulli distribution with a parameter θ. In this case, the expectation-maximization algorithm (EM) by Dempster et al. [1977] can be used to estimate the value of the parameter θ if X or any of its parents are not observed.[4]

The EM algorithm operates by iteratively performing expectation (E) and maximization (M) steps. During the E-step, θ is assumed to be known and fixed and the values of so-called *expected sufficient statistics* (ESS), namely $\mathbb{E}\left[\sum_s \mathcal{I}\left(X = x, \mathcal{P}(X) = \mathbf{p} \mid \mathbf{C}^{(s)}\right)\right]$, are computed,[5] where $\mathbf{C}^{(s)}$ is a vector of observations for a data point s. During the M-step, the new value of

---

[3]By *parents* of a random variable X we mean the set of random variables connected to X by a directed edge in the dependency graph of a model. This set can be empty if there are no edges coming into X.
[4]If X and all its parents are observed, the maximum likelihood estimation can be used instead (see Section 4.1).
[5]See, e.g., [Koller and Friedman, 2009, Section 19.2.2] for more details.

θ is derived using a formula similar to (4.2) to maximize the empirical likelihood. EM starts by assigning some initial values to the model parameters and then repeats the E- and M-steps until convergence.

Notice that the EM algorithm is not guaranteed to converge quickly. The only theoretical guarantee is that the likelihood value improves on each iteration of the algorithm and eventually converges to a (generally local) optimum. In practice, however, the convergence rate is fast, especially in the beginning. It is possible to adopt other optimization techniques, e.g., gradient ascent methods, but we are not going to cover them here.

Below, we show how the EM algorithm can be applied to estimate the parameters of click models. We discuss the E-step in Section 4.2.1, the M-step in Section 4.2.2 and examples of the EM estimation for the UBM and DBN click models in Sections 4.2.3 and 4.2.4, respectively.

4.2.1   EXPECTATION (E-STEP)

Given a click model and a model's parameter θ_c corresponding to a random variable X_c, our goal is to find the value of θ_c that optimizes the log-likelihood of the model given a set of observed query sessions:

$$\mathcal{LL} = \sum_{s \in \mathcal{S}} \log \left(\sum_{\mathbf{X}} P\left(\mathbf{X}, \mathbf{C}^{(s)} \mid \boldsymbol{\Psi}\right) \right), \tag{4.12}$$

where $\mathbf{X}$ is the vector of all hidden variables, $\mathbf{C}^{(s)}$ is the vector of clicks observed in a particular session s and $\boldsymbol{\Psi}$ is the vector of all model parameters.

Generally speaking, the equation above is hard to compute due to the necessity of summing over all hidden variables. As was shown by Dempster et al. [1977], one can replace summation over hidden variables by an expectation. Now instead of the original likelihood function we are going to optimize a similar but different expression:

$$Q = \sum_{s \in \mathcal{S}} \mathbb{E}_{\mathbf{X} \mid \mathbf{C}^{(s)}, \boldsymbol{\Psi}} \left[\log P\left(\mathbf{X}, \mathbf{C}^{(s)} \mid \boldsymbol{\Psi}\right) \right]. \tag{4.13}$$

It simplifies the formula and allows us to group it around the parameter θ_c:

$$\begin{aligned}
Q(\theta_c) &= \sum_{s \in \mathcal{S}} \mathbb{E}_{\mathbf{X} \mid \mathbf{C}^{(s)}, \boldsymbol{\Psi}} \left[\log P\left(\mathbf{X}, \mathbf{C}^{(s)} \mid \boldsymbol{\Psi}\right) \right] \\
&= \sum_{s \in \mathcal{S}} \mathbb{E}_{\mathbf{X} \mid \mathbf{C}^{(s)}, \boldsymbol{\Psi}} \left[\sum_{c_i \in s} \left(\mathcal{I}\left(X_{c_i}^{(s)} = 1, \mathcal{P}(X_{c_i}^{(s)}) = \mathbf{p}\right) \log(\theta_c) + \right. \right. \\
&\qquad\qquad \left. \left. \mathcal{I}\left(X_{c_i}^{(s)} = 0, \mathcal{P}(X_{c_i}^{(s)}) = \mathbf{p}\right) \log(1 - \theta_c) \right) + \mathcal{Z} \right] \\
&= \sum_{s \in \mathcal{S}} \sum_{c_i \in s} \left(P\left(X_{c_i}^{(s)} = 1, \mathcal{P}(X_{c_i}^{(s)}) = \mathbf{p} \mid \mathbf{C}^{(s)}, \boldsymbol{\Psi}\right) \log(\theta_c) + \right.
\end{aligned}$$

$$P\left(X_{c_i}^{(s)} = 0, \mathcal{P}(X_{c_i}^{(s)}) = \mathbf{p} \mid \mathbf{C}^{(s)}, \boldsymbol{\Psi}\right) \log(1 - \theta_c)\right) + \mathcal{Z}, \qquad (4.14)$$

where $\mathcal{P}(X_c) = \mathbf{p}$ is the assignment of the parents of X_c corresponding to the parameter θ_c and $\mathcal{Z}$ is the part of the expression that does not depend on θ_c.

Here, we use the fact that the expectation of a sum is a sum of expectations and the fact that the expected value of an indicator function $\mathbb{E}[\mathcal{I}(expr)]$ is equal to the probability of the corresponding expression $P(expr)$.

So, on the E-step we compute the following expected sufficient statistics:

$$ESS(x) = \sum_{s \in \mathcal{S}} \sum_{c_i \in s} P\left(X_{c_i}^{(s)} = x, \mathcal{P}(X_{c_i}^{(s)}) = \mathbf{p} \mid \mathbf{C}^{(s)}, \boldsymbol{\Psi}\right), \qquad (4.15)$$

where $x \in \{0, 1\}$. The computation is done using formulas from Table 3.1 for each session s.

Notice that at the E-step the value of θ_c is assumed to be known and fixed. Therefore, in order to launch the EM algorithm, θ_c should first be set to some initial value, which will then be updated on every iteration. The initialization of the algorithm is important; it may affect the convergence rate and even push the algorithm to a different local optimum. For example, if the satisfaction probability in DBN (Section 3.8) is initially set to 0, then, as we will see below in Section 4.2.4, Equation 4.41, it will always stay 0.

Existing studies on click models do not provide specific recommendations on choosing initial values and use some intuitive constants, like 0.2 or 0.5. When possible, one should either use values obtained from a simpler model, e.g., a CTR model studied in Section 3.2, or some intuition or prior knowledge.

4.2.2 MAXIMIZATION (M-STEP)

The expected value of the log-likelihood function, obtained during the E-step (Equation 4.14 in Section 4.2.1), should be maximized by taking its derivative with respect to the parameter θ_c and equating it to zero:

$$\frac{\partial Q(\theta_c)}{\partial \theta_c}$$

$$= \sum_{s \in \mathcal{S}} \sum_{c_i \in s} \left(\frac{P\left(X_{c_i}^{(s)} = 1, \mathcal{P}(X_{c_i}^{(s)}) = \mathbf{p} \mid \mathbf{C}^{(s)}, \boldsymbol{\Psi}\right)}{\theta_c} - \frac{P\left(X_{c_i}^{(s)} = 0, \mathcal{P}(X_{c_i}^{(s)}) = \mathbf{p} \mid \mathbf{C}^{(s)}, \boldsymbol{\Psi}\right)}{1 - \theta_c} \right)$$

$$= 0.$$

From this equation the new optimal value of the parameter θ_c can be derived, which will then be used in the next iteration of EM:

$$\theta_c^{(t+1)} = \frac{\sum_{s \in \mathcal{S}} \sum_{c_i \in s} P\left(X_{c_i}^{(s)} = 1, \mathcal{P}(X_{c_i}^{(s)}) = \mathbf{p} \mid \mathbf{C}^{(s)}, \boldsymbol{\Psi}\right)}{\sum_{s \in \mathcal{S}} \sum_{c_i \in s} \sum_{x=0}^{x=1} P\left(X_{c_i}^{(s)} = x, \mathcal{P}(X_{c_i}^{(s)}) = \mathbf{p} \mid \mathbf{C}^{(s)}, \boldsymbol{\Psi}\right)}$$

$$= \frac{\sum_{s \in \mathcal{S}} \sum_{c_i \in s} P\left(X_{c_i}^{(s)} = 1, \mathcal{P}(X_{c_i}^{(s)}) = \mathbf{p} \mid \mathbf{C}^{(s)}, \boldsymbol{\Psi}\right)}{\sum_{s \in \mathcal{S}} \sum_{c_i \in s} P\left(\mathcal{P}(X_{c_i}^{(s)}) = \mathbf{p} \mid \mathbf{C}^{(s)}, \boldsymbol{\Psi}\right)}$$

$$= \frac{ESS^{(t)}(1)}{ESS^{(t)}(1) + ESS^{(t)}(0)}. \tag{4.16}$$

Here, *ESS* is composed of probabilities that should be calculated for each session based on observed clicks $\mathbf{C}^{(s)}$ and a set of parameters $\boldsymbol{\Psi}$ of a click model. Notice that the values of parameters that are calculated during iteration t are used to estimate $\theta_c^{(t+1)}$.

Notice also that it is sometimes practical to smooth the operands in (4.16) in order to deal with data sparsity. For example, Dupret and Piwowarski [2008] added two fictitious observations, one click and one skip (i.e., no click), when estimating the attractiveness probability of each query-document pair. This essentially means that in the numerator the sum starts from 1 instead of 0 and in the denominator it starts from 2.

A slightly more general way to view the smoothing approach is that the parameters themselves have some prior distribution. For example, Chapelle and Zhang [2009] assume that attractiveness and satisfaction parameters of the DBN model have *Beta*(1, 1) priors, which corresponds to the same kind of smoothing discussed above. In general, any prior distributions can be used here. According to Guo et al. [2009a], the right choice of priors and Bayesian approach to parameter learning is crucial for less frequent queries.

Below, we discuss two examples of EM estimation based on the UBM and DBN click models (Sections 4.2.3 and 4.2.4, respectively). To simplify the discussion, we omit the superscript (s), index i and parameter set $\boldsymbol{\Psi}$ in our equations and use r instead of r_u to denote the rank of a document u.

4.2.3   EM ESTIMATION FOR UBM

The UBM click model, introduced in Section 3.5, has two sets of parameters: the attractiveness probability α_{uq} for each query-document pair and the examination probability $\gamma_{rr'}$, which depends on the document rank r and the rank of the previously clicked document r'. In the UBM model, neither the attractiveness A nor the examination E is observed, so we have to use the EM algorithm to estimate the model parameters. Below, we show how to apply the theoretical results presented in Sections 4.2.1 and 4.2.2 to derive the EM update rules for α_{uq} and $\gamma_{rr'}$.

Recall that in order to perform the EM estimation, the model parameters first have to be set to some initial values, which are then updated by the EM algorithm. The original study on UBM suggests to set the attractiveness probabilities to 0.2 and the examination probabilities to 0.5 [Dupret and Piwowarski, 2008].

Attractiveness probability.   According to (3.10) in Section 3.5, the attractiveness probability of the UBM model is defined as follows:

$$\alpha_{uq} = P(A_u = 1).$$ (4.17)

Notice that α_{uq} is defined for sessions that are initiated by the query q and that contain the document u: $\mathcal{S}_{uq} = \{s_q : u \in s_q\}$. Notice, also, that the attractiveness random variable A does not have parents in a Bayesian network, so $P(A_u = 1, \mathcal{P}(A_u) = \mathbf{p} \mid \mathbf{C}) = P(A_u = 1 \mid \mathbf{C})$ and $P(\mathcal{P}(A_u) = \mathbf{p} \mid \mathbf{C}) = 1$. Therefore, we can write the update rule for α_{uq} based on (4.16) as follows:

$$\alpha_{uq}^{(t+1)} = \frac{\sum_{s \in \mathcal{S}_{uq}} P(A_u = 1 \mid \mathbf{C})}{\sum_{s \in \mathcal{S}_{uq}} 1} = \frac{1}{|\mathcal{S}_{uq}|} \sum_{s \in \mathcal{S}_{uq}} P(A_u = 1 \mid \mathbf{C}).$$ (4.18)

The attractiveness event A_u for document u depends on the click event C_u. Therefore, when calculating the attractiveness probability, we can consider two separate cases: the document u is clicked ($C_u = 1$) and the document u is not clicked ($C_u = 0$):

$$
\begin{aligned}
P(A_u = 1 \mid \mathbf{C}) &= P(A_u = 1 \mid C_u) \\
&= \mathcal{I}(C_u = 1)P(A_u = 1 \mid C_u = 1) + \mathcal{I}(C_u = 0)P(A_u = 1 \mid C_u = 0) \\
&= c_u + (1 - c_u)\frac{P(C_u = 0 \mid A_u = 1) \cdot P(A_u - 1)}{P(C_u = 0)} \\
&= c_u + (1 - c_u)\frac{(1 - \gamma_{rr'})\alpha_{uq}}{1 - \gamma_{rr'}\alpha_{uq}}.
\end{aligned}
$$ (4.19)

The first transition holds because C_v and A_u are independent for any document v above u (more formally, for all $r_v < r_u$, $C_v \perp\!\!\!\perp A_u$) and C_w and A_u are conditionally independent given C_u for any document w below u (for all $r_w > r_u$, $C_w \perp\!\!\!\perp A_u \mid C_u$). The second transition splits $P(A_u = 1 \mid C_u)$ into two non-overlapping cases: $C_u = 1$ and $C_u = 0$. For the third transition we observe that if a document is clicked, i.e., $C_u = 1$, then it is attractive, i.e., $A_u = 1$. This means that $P(A_u = 1 \mid C_u = 1) = 1$. In the third transition, we also replace the indicator function $\mathcal{I}(C_u)$ with the actual value c_u, and apply Bayes' rule to $P(A_u = 1 \mid C_u = 0)$. Finally, in the last transition, we calculate probabilities according to the definition of the UBM model, given in (3.9)–(3.14).

Equation 4.19 can be interpreted as follows. If a click is observed for a document, then this document is attractive with probability 1 (first summand). If there is no click on a document, the document is attractive only if it is not examined; the probability of this event is $(1 - \gamma_{rr'})\alpha_{uq}$. The overall probability of no click is $(1 - \gamma_{rr'}\alpha_{uq})$. Then, the probability of a document being attractive, when no click on that document is observed, is the fraction of these two quantities: $(1 - \gamma_{rr'})\alpha_{uq}/(1 - \gamma_{rr'}\alpha_{uq})$ (second summand).

By plugging (4.19) into (4.18) we get the final update rule for the attractiveness parameter α_{uq}:

$$\alpha_{uq}^{(t+1)} = \frac{1}{|\mathcal{S}_{uq}|} \sum_{s \in \mathcal{S}_{uq}} \left(c_u^{(s)} + \left(1 - c_u^{(s)}\right) \frac{\left(1 - \gamma_{rr'}^{(t)}\right)\alpha_{uq}^{(t)}}{1 - \gamma_{rr'}^{(t)}\alpha_{uq}^{(t)}} \right). \qquad (4.20)$$

Notice that in order to calculate the value of α_{uq} in iteration $t + 1$, the values of parameters calculated on the previous iteration t are used. Notice, also, that so far we omitted the superscript (s), but here we show it for completeness.

Examination probability.   In the UBM click model the examination probability is defined as follows (see (3.17) in Section 3.5):

$$\gamma_{rr'} = P(E_r = 1 \mid C_{r'} = 1, C_{r'+1} = 0, \ldots, C_{r-1} = 0), \qquad (4.21)$$

where r' is the rank of the previously clicked document. As we can see, the examination variable E_r depends on all the clicks above r. Thus, the parents of E_r in the UBM Bayesian network are $\mathcal{P}(E_r) = \{C_1, \ldots, C_{r-1}\}$ and the assignment of parents, where $\gamma_{rr'}$ is defined, is

$$\mathbf{p} = [\underbrace{0, \ldots, 0, 1}_{r'}, 0, \ldots, 0]. \qquad (4.22)$$

According to (4.16), we need to compute the expected sufficient statistics (ESS) based on $P(E_r = x, \mathcal{P}(E_r) = \mathbf{p} \mid \mathbf{C})$ where $x = \{0, 1\}$. This probability can be decomposed as follows:

$$P(E_r = x, \mathcal{P}(E_r) = \mathbf{p} \mid \mathbf{C}) = P(E_r = x \mid \mathcal{P}(E_r) = \mathbf{p}, \mathbf{C}) \cdot P(\mathcal{P}(E_r) = \mathbf{p} \mid \mathbf{C}). \qquad (4.23)$$

For sessions where a click at rank r' is observed, but there are no clicks between r' and r, $\mathcal{P}(E_r) = \mathbf{p}$ is always true. We denote this set of sessions as $\mathcal{S}_{rr'} = \{s : c_{r'} = 1, c_{r'+1} = 0, \ldots, c_{r-1} = 0\}$. Therefore, for sessions in $\mathcal{S}_{rr'}$ the components of the ESS can be simplified as follows:

$$P(E_r = x \mid \mathcal{P}(E_r) = \mathbf{p}, \mathbf{C}) = P(E_r = x \mid \mathbf{C}) \qquad (4.24)$$

$$P(\mathcal{P}(E_r) = \mathbf{p} \mid \mathbf{C}) = 1. \qquad (4.25)$$

For all other sessions $P(\mathcal{P}(E_r) = \mathbf{p} \mid \mathbf{C}) = 0$. So, using (4.16) and the above components of the ESS we can write the update rule for $\gamma_{rr'}$ as follows:

$$\gamma_{rr'}^{(t+1)} = \frac{\sum_{s \in \mathcal{S}_{rr'}} P(E_r = 1 \mid \mathbf{C})}{\sum_{s \in \mathcal{S}_{rr'}} 1} = \frac{1}{|\mathcal{S}_{rr'}|} \sum_{s \in \mathcal{S}_{rr'}} P(E_r = 1 \mid \mathbf{C}). \qquad (4.26)$$

Considering the conditional independence $(C_t \perp\!\!\!\perp E_r \mid C_r)$ for $t > r$, the rest of the estimation for the examination probability is similar to that of the attractiveness probability. In particular, the following holds:

$$P(E_r = 1 \mid \mathbf{C}) = c_u + (1 - c_u) \frac{\gamma_{rr'}(1 - \alpha_{uq})}{1 - \gamma_{rr'}\alpha_{uq}}. \qquad (4.27)$$

The interpretation of this equation is similar to that of (4.19).

The final update rule for $\gamma_{rr'}$ can be obtained by combining (4.26) and (4.27) as follows:

$$\gamma_{rr'}^{(t+1)} = \frac{1}{|\mathcal{S}_{rr'}|} \sum_{s \in \mathcal{S}_{rr'}} \left(c_u^{(s)} + \left(1 - c_u^{(s)}\right) \frac{\gamma_{rr'}^{(t)} \left(1 - \alpha_{uq}^{(t)}\right)}{1 - \gamma_{rr'}^{(t)} \alpha_{uq}^{(t)}} \right). \tag{4.28}$$

4.2.4   EM ESTIMATION FOR DBN

The DBN click model (Section 3.8) has two sets of parameters that describe the relevance of a document u, given a query q: attractiveness α_{uq}, also known as perceived relevance, and satisfaction σ_{uq}, also known as actual relevance. In the simplified version of DBN, i.e., SDBN (Section 3.8.1), the corresponding attractiveness and satisfaction random variables are observed and therefore the values of α_{uq} and σ_{uq} can be calculated using MLE, as shown in Section 4.1.3. However, the complete DBN model has an additional parameter γ (continuation probability), which determines if a user continues examining a SERP after they were not satisfied with the current document. In this case, both attractiveness and satisfaction variables of the DBN model are not observable, and so EM estimation should be used to calculate the values of corresponding parameters.

Notice that the original work on DBN admitted that the value of γ could be estimated using EM, but treated it as a configurable parameter [Chapelle and Zhang, 2009]. Here, instead, we show the EM estimation for all parameters of DBN. Notice also that Chapelle and Zhang [2009] derived the attractiveness α_{uq} and satisfaction σ_{uq} using an alternative parameterization (called α and β in the paper) and the forward-backward propagation algorithm. Here, we derive a concise closed-form formula for EM updates for α_{uq} and σ_{uq}.

Recall that we have to set the parameters of DBN to some initial values in order to launch the EM algorithm. Chapelle and Zhang [2009] used 0.5 as the initial value for both α_{uq} and σ_{uq}, while γ was treated as a configurable parameter. Since we estimate γ directly from the data, we may set its initial value to some arbitrary constant, although setting it to some value supposedly close to optimal (0.9 according to Chapelle and Zhang [2009]) may speed up the estimation.

Attractiveness probability.   The attractiveness probability of the DBN click model is defined in a similar way to that of UBM (see (3.35) in Section 3.8):

$$\alpha_{uq} = P(A_u = 1). \tag{4.29}$$

However, unlike the UBM click model, DBN does not explicitly define the examination parameter. According to (3.36)–(3.40) a user examines a document at rank $r + 1$ (that is, $E_{r+1} = 1$) if, and only if, they examine, but are not satisfied with, the document at rank r ($E_r = 1, S_r = 0$). Then, the examination probability of the DBN model can be written recursively as follows:

$$\epsilon_1 = P(E_1 = 1) = 1$$

$$\epsilon_{r+1} = P(E_{r+1} = 1)$$
$$= P(E_{r+1} = 1 \mid E_r = 1) \cdot P(E_r = 1)$$
$$= P(E_{r+1} = 1 \mid E_r = 1) \cdot \epsilon_r$$
$$= \epsilon_r \cdot P(E_{r+1} = 1 \mid S_r = 0, E_r = 1) \cdot P(S_r = 0 \mid E_r = 1)$$
$$= \epsilon_r \gamma \cdot \big(P(S_r = 0 \mid C_{u_r} = 1, E_r = 1) \cdot P(C_{u_r} = 1 \mid E_r = 1) +$$
$$\quad P(S_r = 0 \mid C_{u_r} = 0, E_r = 1) \cdot P(C_{u_r} = 0 \mid E_r = 1) \big)$$
$$= \epsilon_r \gamma \big((1 - \sigma_{u_r q}) \alpha_{u_r q} + (1 - \alpha_{u_r q}) \big). \tag{4.30}$$

This equation can be interpreted as follows. The examination of a document at rank $r + 1$ depends on the examination and click at rank r. If there is a click at rank r (with probability $\alpha_{u_r q}$), then the user examines rank $r + 1$ if they are not satisfied with the document u_r (with probability $1 - \sigma_{u_r q}$) and decides to continue the search (with probability γ). This explains the first summand. If there is no click at rank r (with probability $1 - \alpha_{u_r q}$), then the user continues examining documents with probability γ (second summand).

Now, similarly to UBM, we can apply (4.16) to derive the update rule for the attractiveness parameter α_{uq} of the DBN model:

$$\alpha_{uq}^{(t+1)} = \frac{1}{|\mathcal{S}_{uq}|} \sum_{s \in \mathcal{S}_{uq}} P(A_u = 1 \mid \mathbf{C}), \tag{4.31}$$

where $\mathcal{S}_{uq}$ is the set of sessions initiated by the query q and containing the document u.

As in UBM, the attractiveness probability $P(A_u = 1 \mid \mathbf{C})$ of the DBN model depends on the click event C_u. For example, if a document u is clicked, i.e., $C_u = 1$, then it is attractive, i.e., $A_u = 1$. However, unlike UBM, the DBN model assumes that a user examines documents sequentially and, thus, all documents above the last-clicked one are examined, i.e., for all $r \leq l$, $E_r = 1$, where l is the rank of the last-clicked document. Due to this, the attractiveness probability $P(A_u = 1 \mid \mathbf{C})$ of the DBN model also depends on clicks after the document u. For example, if there are clicks after u, then, according to DBN, u is examined, i.e., $E_{r_u} = 1$. Moreover, if there is no click on u, i.e., $C_u = 0$, then u is certainly not attractive ($A_u = 0$), because it was examined but not clicked.

Let us consider a vector of random variables describing clicks after the document u, and denote it as $\mathbf{C}_{>r}$, where $r = r_u$ for simplicity. The scalar $C_{>r}$ is a binary variable that equals 1 if a click is observed below u and 0 otherwise. Since A_u does not depend on clicks before the document u, the probability of attractiveness in the DBN model can be written as follows:

$$P(A_u = 1 \mid \mathbf{C}) = P(A_u = 1 \mid C_u, \mathbf{C}_{>r})$$
$$= \mathcal{I}(C_u = 1) \cdot P(A_u = 1 \mid C_u = 1, \mathbf{C}_{>r}) +$$
$$\quad \mathcal{I}(C_u = 0) \cdot P(A_u = 1 \mid C_u = 0, \mathbf{C}_{>r})$$

$$= c_u + (1 - c_u) \cdot$$
$$\left(\mathcal{I}(C_{>r} = 1) \cdot P(A_u = 1 \mid C_u = 0, C_{>r} = 1, \mathbf{C}_{>r}) + \right.$$
$$\left. \mathcal{I}(C_{>r} = 0) \cdot P(A_u = 1 \mid C_u = 0, C_{>r} = 0, \mathbf{C}_{>r}) \right)$$
$$= c_u + (1 - c_u)(1 - c_{>r}) \cdot$$
$$\frac{P(C_u = 0, C_{>r} = 0 \mid A_u = 1) \cdot P(A_u = 1)}{P(C_u = 0, C_{>r} = 0)}. \tag{4.32}$$

Here, we first distinguish two cases: $C_u = 1$ and $C_u = 0$. If a click on u is observed, i.e., $C_u = 1$, then u is attractive and other clicks below u do not matter, i.e., $P(A_u = 1 \mid C_u = 1, \mathbf{C}_{>r}) = 1$. In the second transition, we split the equation based on clicks after u: $C_{>r} = 1$ and $C_{>r} = 0$. If u is not clicked, i.e., $C_u = 0$, but there are clicks after u, i.e., $C_{>r} = 1$, then u is not attractive, because it was examined but not clicked: $P(A_u = 1 \mid C_u = 0, C_{>r} = 1, \mathbf{C}_{>r}) = 0$. Finally, in the last transition, we use the fact that $C_{>r} = 0$ is the same as $\mathbf{C}_{>r} = \mathbf{0}$ and apply Bayes' rule to $P(A_u = 1 \mid C_u = 0, C_{>r} = 0)$.

In (4.32), we need to calculate two probabilities: $P(C_u = 0, C_{>r} = 0 \mid A_u = 1)$ and $P(C_u = 0, C_{>r} = 0)$. First, an attractive document u is not clicked only if it is not examined:

$$P(C_u = 0, C_{>r} = 0 \mid A_u = 1) = P(C_u = 0, C_{>r} = 0 \mid A_u = 1, E_r = 0) \cdot P(E_r = 0)$$
$$= P(E_r = 0) = 1 - \epsilon_r. \tag{4.33}$$

Second, the probability $P(C_u = 0, C_{>r} = 0) = P(C_{\geq r} = 0)$ can be computed as $1 - P(C_{\geq r} = 1)$, while $P(C_{\geq r} = 1)$ can be calculated based on the definition of the DBN model, given in (3.34)–(3.40):

$$P(C_{\geq r} = 1) = \epsilon_r \cdot X_r, \tag{4.34}$$

where

$$X_r = P(C_{\geq r} = 1 \mid E_r = 1)$$
$$= P(C_r = 1 \mid E_r = 1) + P(C_r = 0, C_{\geq r+1} = 1 \mid E_r = 1)$$
$$= \alpha_{u_r q} + P(C_{\geq r+1} = 1 \mid C_r = 0, E_r = 1) \cdot P(C_r = 0 \mid E_r = 1)$$
$$= \alpha_{u_r q} + P(C_{\geq r+1} = 1 \mid E_{r+1} = 1) \cdot P(E_{r+1} = 1 \mid C_r = 0, E_r = 1) \cdot (1 - \alpha_{u_r q})$$
$$= \alpha_{u_r q} + (1 - \alpha_{u_r q}) \gamma X_{r+1}. \tag{4.35}$$

We assume that $X_{N+1} = 0$, where N is the size of the SERP (usually 10).

Combining (4.31)–(4.35), we get the final update rule for the attractiveness parameter α_{uq}:

$$\alpha_{uq}^{(t+1)} = \frac{1}{|\mathcal{S}_{uq}|} \sum_{s \in \mathcal{S}_{uq}} \left(c_u^{(s)} + \left(1 - c_u^{(s)} \right) \left(1 - c_{>r}^{(s)} \right) \frac{\left(1 - \epsilon_r^{(t)} \right) \alpha_{uq}^{(t)}}{1 - \epsilon_r^{(t)} X_r^{(t)}} \right), \tag{4.36}$$

where ϵ_r is given in (4.30) and X_r is given by the recursive formula (4.35).

Satisfaction probability.   According to (3.38) in Section 3.8, the satisfaction probability of the DBN model is defined as follows:

$$\sigma_{uq} = P(S_u = 1 \mid C_u = 1). \tag{4.37}$$

That is, σ_{uq} is defined only for clicked documents. In other words, the parent of S_u is $\mathcal{P}(S_u) = C_u$ and the assignment of $\mathcal{P}(S_u)$ for which σ_{uq} is defined is $\mathbf{p} = [1]$.

According to (4.16), we need to compute the expected sufficient statistics based on $P(S_u = x, C_u = 1 \mid \mathbf{C})$, where $x = \{0, 1\}$. Similarly to the UBM examination probability (Section 4.2.3), this probability simplifies to $P(S_u = x \mid \mathbf{C})$ for sessions, where a click on the document u is observed. We will denote these sessions as $\mathcal{S}'_{uq} = \{s : s \in \mathcal{S}_{uq}, c_u^{(s)} = 1\}$.

Then, according to (4.16), the update rule for σ_{uq} can be written as follows:

$$\sigma_{uq}^{(t+1)} = \frac{\sum_{s \in \mathcal{S}'_{uq}} P(S_u = 1 \mid \mathbf{C})}{\sum_{s \in \mathcal{S}'_{uq}} 1}$$

$$= \frac{1}{|\mathcal{S}'_{uq}|} \sum_{s \in \mathcal{S}'_{uq}} P(S_u = 1 \mid \mathbf{C}). \tag{4.38}$$

Given the fact that $c_u = 1$ for all sessions $s \in \mathcal{S}'_{uq}$, the satisfaction probability σ_{uq} does not depend on clicks above the document u. If a click is observed below u, i.e., $C_{>r_u} = 1$, then the user is not satisfied with u, i.e., $S_u = 0$. Otherwise, there are no clicks after the document u. In other words, the probability of satisfaction $P(S_u = 1 \mid \mathbf{C})$ depends on C_u and on $\mathbf{C}_{>r_u}$ (the vector of observed clicks after rank r_u). So $P(S_u = 1 \mid \mathbf{C})$ can be written as follows:

$$\begin{aligned} P(S_u = 1 \mid \mathbf{C}) &= P(S_u = 1 \mid C_u = 1, \mathbf{C}_{>r}) \\ &= \mathcal{I}(C_{>r} = 1) \cdot P(S_u = 1 \mid C_u = 1, C_{>r} = 1, \mathbf{C}_{>r}) + \\ &\quad \mathcal{I}(C_{>r} = 0) \cdot P(S_u = 1 \mid C_u = 1, C_{>r} = 0, \mathbf{C}_{>r}) \\ &= (1 - c_{>r}) \cdot P(S_u = 1 \mid C_u = 1, C_{>r} = 0) \\ &= (1 - c_{>r}) \cdot \frac{P(C_{>r} = 0 \mid S_u = 1, C_u = 1) \cdot P(S_u = 1 \mid C_u = 1)}{P(C_{>r} = 0 \mid C_u = 1)} \\ &= (1 - c_{>r}) \cdot \frac{\sigma_{uq}}{P(C_{>r} = 0 \mid C_u = 1)}. \end{aligned} \tag{4.39}$$

In the second transition, we consider two cases: $C_{>r} = 1$ and $C_{>r} = 0$. In the third transition, we note that $P(S_u = 1 \mid C_{>r} = 1) = 0$, because, according to the DBN model, a user cannot be satisfied with a document u if they click on other documents below u. Then we also apply Bayes' rule to $P(S_u = 1 \mid C_u = 1, C_{>r} = 0)$. Finally, in the last transition, we note that $P(C_{>r} = 0 \mid S_u = 1, C_u = 1) = 1$, because if a user is satisfied with u then they do not examine other documents. We also replace the probability of satisfaction $P(S_u = 1 \mid C_u = 1)$ with the corresponding parameter σ_{uq}.

In (4.39), we still need to calculate the probability of no click after a document u, i.e., $P(C_{>r} = 0 \mid C_u = 1) = P(C_{\geq r+1} = 0 \mid C_u = 1)$. It can be calculated as $1 - P(C_{\geq r+1} = 1 \mid C_u = 1)$ where the last term is related to X given by (4.35):

$$P(C_{\geq r+1} = 1 \mid C_u = 1) = P(C_{\geq r+1} = 1 \mid E_{r+1} = 1) \cdot P(E_{r+1} = 1 \mid C_u = 1)$$
$$= X_{r+1} \cdot (1 - \sigma_{u_r q})\gamma. \tag{4.40}$$

Then, the final update rule for σ_{uq} can be written as follows:

$$\sigma_{uq}^{(t+1)} = \frac{1}{|S'_{uq}|} \sum_{s \in S'_{uq}} \left(1 - c_{>r}^{(s)}\right) \frac{\sigma_{uq}^{(t)}}{1 - \left(1 - \sigma_{u_r q}^{(t)}\right)\gamma^{(t)} X_{r+1}^{(t)}}, \tag{4.41}$$

where X is given by (4.35).

Continuation probability. The continuation probability γ in the DBN model is defined as follows (see (3.40) in Section 3.8):

$$\gamma = P(E_{r+1} = 1 \mid E_r = 1, S_{u_r} = 0), \tag{4.42}$$

where neither of E_{r+1}, E_r and S_{u_r} is observed. Here, the parents of E_{r+1} are $\mathcal{P}(E_{r+1}) = \{E_r, S_{u_r}\}$ and their assignment for which γ is defined is $\mathbf{p} = [1, 0]$.

According to (4.16), we need to compute the expected sufficient statistics $ESS(z) = \sum_{s \in S} \sum_r P(E_{r+1} = z, E_r = 1, S_{u_r} = 0 \mid \mathbf{C})$, where $z = \{0, 1\}$. There is no *concise* closed-form formula for this statistic. In order to compute it, we introduce an additional factor:

$$\Phi(x, y, z) = \frac{P(E_r = x, S_{u_r} = y, E_{r+1} = z, \mathbf{C})}{P(\mathbf{C}_{<r})}. \tag{4.43}$$

Once we have computed this factor we can compute the ESS as follows:

$$ESS(z) = \sum_{s \in S} \sum_r P(E_{r+1} = z, E_r = 1, S_{u_r} = 0 \mid \mathbf{C})$$

$$= \sum_{s \in S} \sum_r \frac{P(E_{r+1} = z, E_r = 1, S_{u_r} = 0, \mathbf{C})}{P(\mathbf{C})}$$

$$= \sum_{s \in S} \sum_r \frac{P(E_{r+1} = z, E_r = 1, S_{u_r} = 0, \mathbf{C})}{\sum_x \sum_y \sum_z P(E_{r+1} = z, E_r = x, S_{u_r} = y, \mathbf{C})}$$

$$= \sum_{s \in S} \sum_r \frac{P(E_{r+1} = z, E_r = 1, S_{u_r} = 0, \mathbf{C}) \cdot \frac{1}{P(\mathbf{C}_{<r})}}{\sum_x \sum_y \sum_z P(E_{r+1} = z, E_r = x, S_{u_r} = y, \mathbf{C}) \cdot \frac{1}{P(\mathbf{C}_{<r})}}$$

$$= \sum_{s \in S} \sum_r \frac{\Phi^{(s)}(1, 0, z)}{\sum_x \sum_y \sum_z \Phi^{(s)}(x, y, z)} \tag{4.44}$$

We compute the factor $\Phi(x, y, z)$ using the chain rule for probabilities and the cascade nature of the model, which guarantees that events at ranks greater than or equal to r are conditionally independent of the clicks $\mathbf{C}_{<r}$ above r given examination E_r:

$$\Phi(x, y, z) = P(E_r = x, C_r = c_r, S_{u_r} = y, E_{r+1} = z, \mathbf{C}_{\geq r+1} \mid \mathbf{C}_{<r})$$

$$= P(E_r = x \mid \mathbf{C}_{<r}) \cdot P(C_r = c_r \mid E_r = x) \cdot P(S_r = y \mid C_r = c_r) \cdot$$

$$P(E_{r+1} = z \mid E_r = x, S_r = y, C_r = c_r) \cdot P(\mathbf{C}_{\geq r+1} \mid E_{r+1} = z). \quad (4.45)$$

The first multiplier is computed as follows:

$$P(E_r = x \mid \mathbf{C}_{<r}) = \begin{cases} P(E_r = 1 \mid \mathbf{C}_{<r}) & \text{if } x = 1 \\ 1 - P(E_r = 1 \mid \mathbf{C}_{<r}) & \text{if } x = 0, \end{cases} \quad (4.46)$$

where $P(E_r = 1 \mid \mathbf{C}_{<r})$ is given by the recursive formula (3.48) and is presented in the Table 3.1. The last multiplier is computed as follows:

$$P(\mathbf{C}_{\geq r+1} \mid E_{r+1} = z) = \begin{cases} P(\mathbf{C}_{\geq r+1} \mid E_{r+1} = 1) & \text{if } z = 1 \\ 1 & \text{if } z = 0 \text{ and } \mathbf{C}_{\geq r+1} = \mathbf{0} \quad (4.47) \\ 0 & \text{otherwise} \end{cases}$$

If $z = 0$, it either equals 1 if there are no clicks after r ($\mathbf{C}_{\geq r+1} = \mathbf{0}$) or 0 otherwise. If, in turn, $z = 1$, then $P(\mathbf{C}_{\geq r+1} \mid E_{r+1} = 1)$ is computed using the chain rule of probabilities and the model formulas (3.34)–(3.40).

The other multipliers in (4.45), namely $P(C_r = c_r \mid E_r = x)$, $P(S_r = y \mid C_r = c_r)$ and $P(E_{r+1} = z \mid E_r = x, S_r = y, C_r = c_r)$, are computed directly from the model formulas (3.34)–(3.40).

4.3   FORMULAS FOR CLICK MODEL PARAMETERS

In this chapter we have presented two main methods used to estimate parameters of click models, namely maximum likelihood estimation and expectation-maximization. We have also shown how these methods can be used to calculate the parameters of the models that were presented in Chapter 3. Table 4.1 summarizes the MLE and EM formulas derived throughout this chapter. The table shows the abbreviation of each click model, the estimation algorithm that should be used (MLE or EM), the list of parameters and the corresponding MLE formulas or EM update rules.

Recall that $c_u^{(s)}$ denotes an actual click on a document u in a search session s, where $c_u^{(s)} = 1$ if there was a click on u and 0 otherwise. Recall also that the EM update rules use values of parameters that were calculated during iteration t (e.g., $\gamma^{(t)}$), to compute new values during iteration $t + 1$ (e.g., $\gamma^{(t+1)}$). In Table 4.1 we use r instead of r_u to simplify the notation. For other notation used in Table 4.1, please refer to Table 2.1 in Chapter 2.

Table 4.1: Formulas for calculating parameters of click models. For each model the table shows its abbreviation, parameter estimation algorithm (MLE/EM), list of parameters and corresponding MLE formulas or EM update rules (*Continues.*)

Click model	Estimation algorithm	Parameters	Formula
RCM	MLE	ρ	$\rho = \dfrac{1}{\sum_{s\in S}|s|}\sum_{s\in S}\sum_{u\in s}c_u^{(s)}$
RCTR	MLE	ρ_r	$\rho_r = \dfrac{1}{|S|}\sum_{s\in S}c_r^{(s)}$
DCTR	MLE	ρ_{uq}	$\rho_{uq} = \dfrac{1}{|S_{uq}|}\sum_{s\in S_{uq}}c_u^{(s)}$, where $S_{uq}=\{s_q : u \in s_q\}$
PBM	EM	α_{uq}	$\alpha_{uq}^{(t+1)} = \dfrac{1}{|S_{uq}|}\sum_{s\in S_{uq}}\left(c_u^{(s)} + (1-c_u^{(s)})\dfrac{(1-\gamma_r^{(t)})\alpha_{uq}^{(t)}}{1-\gamma_r^{(t)}\alpha_{uq}^{(t)}}\right)$, where $S_{uq}=\{s_q : u \in s_q\}$
		γ_r	$\gamma_r^{(t+1)} = \dfrac{1}{|S|}\sum_{s\in S}\left(c_u^{(s)} + (1-c_u^{(s)})\dfrac{(1-\alpha_{uq}^{(t)})\gamma_r^{(t)}}{1-\gamma_r^{(t)}\alpha_{uq}^{(t)}}\right)$
CM	MLE	α_{uq}	$\alpha_{uq} = \dfrac{1}{|S_{uq}|}\sum_{s\in S_{uq}}c_u^{(s)}$, where $S_{uq}=\{s_q : u \in s_q, r_u \le l\}$, l is the rank of the first-clicked document
UBM	EM	α_{uq}	$\alpha_{uq}^{(t+1)} = \dfrac{1}{|S_{uq}|}\sum_{s\in S_{uq}}\left(c_u^{(s)} + (1-c_u^{(s)})\dfrac{(1-\gamma_{rr'}^{(t)})\alpha_{uq}^{(t)}}{1-\gamma_{rr'}^{(t)}\alpha_{uq}^{(t)}}\right)$, where $S_{uq}=\{s_q : u \in s_q\}$
		$\gamma_{rr'}$	$\gamma_{rr'}^{(t+1)} = \dfrac{1}{|S_{rr'}|}\sum_{s\in S_{rr'}}\left(c_u^{(s)} + (1-c_u^{(s)})\dfrac{(1-\alpha_{uq}^{(t)})\gamma_{rr'}^{(t)}}{1-\gamma_{rr'}^{(t)}\alpha_{uq}^{(t)}}\right)$, where $S_{rr'}=\{s : c_r^{(s)}=1, c_{r'+1}^{(s)}=0,\ldots,c_{r-1}^{(s)}=0\}$
SDCM	MLE	α_{uq}	$\alpha_{uq} = \dfrac{1}{|S_{uq}|}\sum_{s\in S_{uq}}c_u^{(s)}$, where $S_{uq}=\{s_q : u \in s_q, r_u \le l\}$, l is the rank of the last-clicked document
		λ_r	$\lambda_r = \dfrac{1}{|S_r|}\sum_{s\in S_r}\mathcal{I}(r\neq l)$, where $S_r=\{s : c_{u_r}^{(s)}=1\}$

Table 4.1: *(Continued.)* Formulas for calculating parameters of click models. For each model the table shows its abbreviation, parameter estimation algorithm (MLE/EM), list of parameters and corresponding MLE formulas or EM update rules *(Continues.)*

CCM EM α_{uq}

$$\alpha_{uq}^{(t+1)} = \frac{1}{|S_{uq}| + |S'_{uq}|} \sum_{s \in S_{uq}} \left(c_u^{(s)} + (1 - c_u^{(s)})(1 - c_{>r}^{(s)}) \frac{(1-\epsilon_r^{(t)})\alpha_{uq}^{(t)}}{1-\epsilon_r^{(t)} Y_r^{(t)}} \right) +$$

$$\frac{1}{|S_{uq}| + |S'_{uq}|} \sum_{s \in S'_{uq}} (1 - c_{>r}^{(s)}) \frac{\alpha_{uq}^{(t)}}{1 - \left(\tau_2\left(1-\alpha_{u,r-q}^{(t)}\right) + \tau_3\alpha_{u,r-q}^{(t)}\right) Y_{r+1}^{(t)}},$$

where $S_{uq} = \{s_q : u \in s_q\}$, $S'_{uq} = \{s : s \in S_{uq}, c_u^{(s)} = 1\}$,

$\epsilon_{r+1}^{(t)} = \epsilon_r^{(t)} \left(\left(1-\alpha_{u,r-q}^{(t)}\right)\tau_1 + \alpha_{u,r-q}^{(t)} \left(\tau_2\left(1-\alpha_{u,r-q}^{(t)}\right) + \tau_3\alpha_{u,r-q}^{(t)}\right) \right)$,

$Y_r^{(t)} = P(C_{\geq r} = 1 \,|\, E_r = 1) = \alpha_{u,r-q}^{(t)} + \left(1-\alpha_{u,r-q}^{(t)}\right)\tau_1^{(t)} Y_{r+1}^{(t)},\ Y_{N+1}^{(t)} = 0$,

$c_{>r}^{(s)} = 1$ if in the session s a click is observed after rank r, and 0 otherwise

τ_1 $\tau_1^{(t+1)} = \frac{ESS^{(t)}(1)}{ESS^{(t)}(1)+ESS^{(t)}(0)}$, $ESS(z) = \sum_{s \in S} \sum_{r:c_r^{(s)}=0} \frac{\sum_y \Phi^{(s)}(1,y,z)}{\Phi^{(s)}(1,0,z)}$,

τ_2 $\tau_2^{(t+1)} = \frac{ESS^{(t)}(1)}{ESS^{(t)}(1)+ESS^{(t)}(0)}$, $ESS(z) = \sum_{s \in S} \sum_{r:c_r^{(s)}=1} \frac{\sum_y \Phi^{(s)}(1,y,z)}{\Phi^{(s)}(1,y,z)}$,

τ_3 $\tau_3^{(t+1)} = \frac{ESS^{(t)}(1)}{ESS^{(t)}(1)+ESS^{(t)}(0)}$, $ESS(z) = \sum_{s \in S} \sum_{r:c_r^{(s)}=1} \frac{\sum_x\sum_y\sum_z \Phi^{(s)}(x,y,z)}{\Phi^{(s)}(1,1,z)}$,

where Φ is defined by (4.43) and computed using (4.45)

DBN EM α_{uq}

$$\alpha_{uq}^{(t+1)} = \frac{1}{|S_{uq}|} \sum_{s \in S_{uq}} \left(c_u^{(s)} + (1 - c_u^{(s)})(1 - c_{>r}^{(s)}) \frac{(1-\epsilon_r^{(t)})\alpha_{uq}^{(t)}}{1-\epsilon_r^{(t)} X_r^{(t)}} \right),$$

where $S_{uq} = \{s_q : u \in s_q\}$, $\epsilon_{r+1}^{(t)} = \epsilon_r^{(t)} \gamma^{(t)} \left(\left(1-\sigma_{u,r-q}^{(t)}\right)\alpha_{u,r-q}^{(t)} + \left(1-\alpha_{u,r-q}^{(t)}\right) \right)$,

$X_r^{(t)} = P(C_{\geq r} = 1 \,|\, E_r = 1) = \alpha_{u,r-q}^{(t)} + \left(1-\alpha_{u,r-q}^{(t)}\right)\gamma^{(t)} X_{r+1}^{(t)},\ X_{N+1}^{(t)} = 0$,

$c_{>r}^{(s)} = 1$ if in the session s a click is observed after rank r, and 0 otherwise

σ_{uq} $\sigma_{uq}^{(t+1)} = \frac{1}{|S'_{uq}|} \sum_{s \in S'_{uq}} \left(1 - c_{>r}^{(s)}\right) \frac{\sigma_{uq}^{(t)}}{1-\left(1-\sigma_{u,r-q}^{(t)}\right)\gamma^{(t)} X_{r+1}^{(t)}}$,

where $S'_{uq} = \{s : s \in S_{uq}, c_u^{(s)} = 1\}$ and X is defined above

γ $\gamma^{(t+1)} = \frac{ESS^{(t)}(1)}{ESS^{(t)}(1)+ESS^{(t)}(0)}$, $ESS(z) = \sum_{s \in S} \sum_r \frac{\Phi^{(s)}(1,0,z)}{\sum_x\sum_y\sum_z \Phi^{(s)}(x,y,z)}$,

where Φ is defined by (4.43) and computed using (4.45)

Table 4.1: *(Continued.)* Formulas for calculating parameters of click models. For each model the table shows its abbreviation, parameter estimation algorithm (MLE/EM), list of parameters and corresponding MLE formulas or EM update rules

SDBN	MLE	α_{uq}	$\alpha_{uq} = \frac{1}{	\mathcal{S}_{uq}	} \sum_{s \in \mathcal{S}_{uq}} c_u^{(s)}$,
			where $\mathcal{S}_{uq} = \{s_q : u \in s_q, r_u \leq l\}$, l is the rank of the last-clicked document
		σ_{uq}	$\sigma_{uq} = \frac{1}{	\mathcal{S}'_{uq}	} \sum_{s \in \mathcal{S}'_{uq}} \mathcal{I}(r_u^{(s)} = l)$,
			where $\mathcal{S}'_{uq} = \left\{ s_q : u \in s_q, r_u \leq l, c_u^{(s)} = 1 \right\}$

4.4   ALTERNATIVE ESTIMATION METHODS

As an alternative to estimation based on MLE or EM, a Bayesian approach is sometimes used. Two notable examples are the so-called *Bayesian browsing model* (BBM) [Liu et al., 2009] and the *hierarchical models* (H-UBM, H-CCM, H-DBN) of Zhang et al. [2010]. Both approaches make additional assumptions about prior distributions for model parameters and are reported to run faster than the EM estimation and to outperform EM-trained models, especially for queries that rarely occur in the training set.

The BBM model by Liu et al. [2009] is essentially a UBM model (Section 3.5), where the attractiveness α_{uq} is assumed to have a uniform prior distribution. The $\gamma_{rr'}$ parameters can then be computed in a closed form by maximizing the likelihood (which in this case does not depend on α_{uq}). In turn, the α_{uq} parameters are not estimated directly, but their posterior distribution is derived instead. This allows for better flexibility, as one may either use this posterior distribution or use expected values for each α_{uq}.

The hierarchical models by Zhang et al. [2010] assume that all model parameters have a normal prior distribution. With each session added to a training set, the posterior distribution is computed and approximated with another normal distribution (a process referred to as Gaussian density filtering). This approximated distribution replaces the parameter distribution estimated at a previous step and then the process continues. The authors also suggest a modification to their estimation process called *deep probit Bayesian inference*, which adds feature-based smoothing based on, e.g., BM25 query-document matching scores. This allows for more accurate estimations in cases where the data is too sparse.

Shen et al. [2012] suggest to adopt the ideas of collaborative filtering to the click modeling problem. While the main focus of the authors is on user personalization (see Section 8.3), their first idea of matrix factorization already leads to a substantial improvement of the model quality as measured by the log-likelihood (Section 5.1). The MFCM model that they propose (*matrix factorization click model*) introduces Gaussian priors for the model parameters and adopts a different estimation process based on matrix factorization. The performance improvement is achieved by the fact that previously unseen documents now get better estimations based on other elements in the decomposed parameter matrix.

Now that we have introduced the basic click models as well as estimation methods for working with them, we are almost ready to evaluate those models. Next, in Chapter 5, we introduce different evaluation methods for click models, and in Chapter 6 we list available datasets before turning to experiments in Chapter 7.

CHAPTER 5

Evaluation

Evaluation lies at the core of any scientific method and click models are no exception. We want to be sure that by introducing a more complex model we do, in fact, obtain better results. In this chapter we discuss different ways to evaluate click models. We start with traditional statistical evaluation approaches, such as log-likelihood and perplexity, and then discuss more application-oriented evaluation methods like click-through rate prediction, and evaluation based on NDCG and intuitiveness.

5.1 LOG-LIKELIHOOD

Whenever we have a statistical model, we can evaluate its accuracy by looking at the likelihood of some held-out test set (see, e.g., [Fisher, 1922]). For each session in the test set S we compute how likely this session is according to our click model:

$$\mathcal{L}(s) = P_M\left(C_1 = c_1^{(s)}, \ldots, C_n = c_n^{(s)}\right), \tag{5.1}$$

where P_M is the probability measure induced by the click model M. If we further assume independence of sessions, we can compute the logarithm of the joint likelihood:

$$\mathcal{LL}(M) = \sum_{s \in S} \log P_M\left(C_1 = c_1^{(s)}, \ldots, C_n = c_n^{(s)}\right). \tag{5.2}$$

This metric is known as *log-likelihood* and usually computed using the formula of total probability:

$$\mathcal{LL}(M) = \sum_{s \in S} \sum_{r=1}^{n} \log P_M\left(C_r = c_r^{(s)} \mid \mathbf{C}_{<r} = \mathbf{c}_{<r}^{(s)}\right). \tag{5.3}$$

As a logarithm of a probability measure this metric always has non-positive values with higher values representing better prediction quality. The log-likelihood of a perfect prediction equals 0.

5.2 PERPLEXITY

Craswell et al. [2008] proposed to use the notion of *cross-entropy* from information theory [Murphy, 2013] as a metric for click models. This metric was not easy to interpret and it did not become widely used. Instead, Dupret and Piwowarski [2008] proposed to use the conceptually similar notion of *perplexity* as a metric for assessing click models:

$$p_r(M) = 2^{-\frac{1}{|S|} \sum_{s \in S} \left(c_r^{(s)} \log_2 q_r^{(s)} + \left(1 - c_r^{(s)}\right) \log_2 \left(1 - q_r^{(s)}\right) \right)}, \tag{5.4}$$

where $q_r^{(s)}$ is the probability of a user clicking the document at rank r in the session s as predicted by the model M, i.e., $q_r^{(s)} = P_M(C_r = 1 \mid q, \mathbf{u})$. Note that while computing this probability only the query q and the vector of documents $\mathbf{u}$ are used and not the clicks in the session s. Usually, perplexity is reported for each rank r independently, but it is also often averaged across ranks to have an overall measure of model quality:

$$p(M) = \frac{1}{n} \sum_{r=1}^{n} p_r(M). \tag{5.5}$$

Notice that perplexity of the ideal prediction is 1. Indeed, an ideal model would predict the click probability q_r to be always equal to the actual click c_r (zero or one). On the other hand, the perplexity of the simple Random Click Model with probability $\rho = 0.5$ (Section 3.1) is equal to 2. Hence, the perplexity of a realistic model should lie between 1 and 2.[1]

Notice, also, that better models have lower values of perplexity. When we compare perplexity scores of two models A and B, we follow Guo et al. [2009a] and compute the *perplexity gain* of A over B as follows:

$$gain(A, B) = \frac{p^B - p^A}{p^B - 1}. \tag{5.6}$$

The perplexity is typically higher for top documents and decreases toward the bottom of a SERP.[2] As we will see later, predicting a click is generally much harder than predicting its absence and, since top documents typically get more clicks, they are harder for a click model to get right.

5.2.1   CONDITIONAL PERPLEXITY

One of the building blocks of perplexity is the click probability q_r at rank r. In the above definition we defined it as the full probability $P(C_r = 1)$. This probability is independent of the clicks in the current session s and could be tricky to compute as it involves marginalizing over all possible assignments for previous clicks $\mathbf{C}_{<r}$.

Another possibility for defining perplexity is to use the conditional click probability, given the previous clicks in the session. We introduce another version of perplexity, which we call *conditional perplexity*:

$$\tilde{p}_r(M) = 2^{-\frac{1}{|S|} \sum_{s \in S} \left(c_r^{(s)} \log_2 \tilde{q}_r^{(s)} + \left(1 - c_r^{(s)}\right) \log_2 \left(1 - \tilde{q}_r^{(s)}\right) \right)}, \tag{5.7}$$

---

[1]One can also obtain tighter upper bounds using the RCTR model (Section 3.2.1) [Dupret and Piwowarski, 2008].

[2]As was shown in [Chuklin et al., 2013d], this does not hold beyond the first SERP. In particular, when a search interface provides pagination buttons to switch to a second or further SERP (i.e., retrieve the next ranked group of documents) the perplexity no longer decreases with rank.

where $\tilde{q}_r^{(s)}$ is the conditional probability:

$$\tilde{q}_r^{(s)} = P_M \left(C_r = 1 \mid C_1 = c_1^{(s)}, \ldots C_{r-1} = c_{r-1}^{(s)} \right). \tag{5.8}$$

Unlike the original version of perplexity (5.4), which evaluates a model's ability to predict clicks without any input, the conditional perplexity is just a decomposition of the likelihood (Section 5.1) and also factors in a model's ability to exploit clicks above the current rank. Since the conditional perplexity uses the beginning of a session $\mathbf{c}_{<r}^{(s)}$ to compute the probability $\tilde{q}_r^{(s)}$ it typically yields lower values than the regular perplexity, especially for models like UBM (Section 3.5) that rely on the accuracy of previous clicks. It is important to keep this in mind when comparing results from different publications using different versions of perplexity.

5.2.2 DETAILED PERPLEXITY ANALYSIS

Clicks and skips. Dupret and Piwowarski [2008] suggest that one should look separately at perplexity of predicting clicks ($c_r = 1$) and perplexity of predicting "non-clicks" or *skips* ($c_r = 0$). This perspective reveals some general trends about click models and helps to better compare them to each other. The authors show that predicting skips is usually much easier than predicting clicks. This is due to the fact that the majority of documents are not clicked and even a simple random click model with a small value of the parameter ρ can bring perplexity close to 1 for skips. This breakdown has also been used in [Chuklin et al., 2013d] to show how two different variations of a model outperform one another on either clicks or skips.

Query frequency stratification. Guo et al. [2009a,b] analyze perplexity values for different query frequency buckets. Naturally, user behavior can be modeled more accurately for frequent queries, i.e., queries that appear many times in a training set. Following this evaluation approach, one may be interested to determine whether some frequency buckets are particularly hard to model. This method also allows one to compare how different click models handle the sparsity of data.

5.3 CLICK-THROUGH RATE PREDICTION

Click-through rate (or CTR for short) is a ratio of the cases when a particular document was clicked to the cases when it was shown. CTRs are often used to compare ranking methods in A/B-testing (see, e.g., [Kohavi et al., 2008]) and, even more importantly, when evaluating sponsored search. Predicting clicks in sponsored search [Richardson et al., 2007] has an immense influence on revenue and is often done using click models (see, e.g., [Ashkan and Clarke, 2012, Zhu et al., 2010]). Below we discuss two ways of evaluating predictive power of a click model in terms of CTR.

Removing position bias. Chapelle and Zhang [2009] evaluate CTR prediction using the assumption that there is no position effect on the first position. In other words, if there is a model that predicts the probability of a click given examination $P(C_u = 1 \mid E_u = 1)$, that value would be equal to the click-through rate $P(C_u = 1)$ if u is on the first position ($r_u = 1$). This means that by placing the document on top, we remove the position bias. To do that, Chapelle and Zhang suggest the following procedure:

1. Consider document u appearing on both the first position and some other position for the same query (but in different sessions).

2. Use sessions where u appears on the first position as a test set and the rest of the sessions as a training set.

3. Perform parameter estimation using the training set.

4. Estimate $P(C_u = 1 \mid E_u = 1)$ from the training set and compare these values to the CTR values obtained from the test set.

To compare CTR values two metrics have been suggested: Mean Square Error (MSE) and Kullback-Leibler (KL) divergence [Kullback and Leibler, 1951].

   While this method directly evaluates CTR, it uses a very skewed set of queries. First, it only looks at previously seen query-document pairs and does not evaluate the generalization ability of the model. Second, for each document it requires sessions where the document appears on the first position and sessions where the document appears on other positions. While this naturally happens in major search engine systems due to user experiments and personalization effects (see, e.g., [Radlinski and Craswell, 2013]), it is not guaranteed to be the case for other search systems. Moreover, these high-variability queries represent a special set of queries that is not representative of the whole distribution.

Direct CTR estimation.   Zhu et al. [2010] suggest an alternative method where CTR is estimated by simulating user clicks multiple times and comparing simulated CTR values to the real ones.[3] CTR is computed for each triple (u, q, s) consisting of a document u, a query q and a session s that was initiated by the query q and contains the document u. While simulated CTR is a real value computed by repeatedly generating clicks given a query and a SERP, the real CTR is either equal to 1 if the document was clicked or equal to 0 otherwise. To avoid comparing real-valued simulated CTRs to binary-valued actual CTRs, Zhu et al. [2010] suggest the following method. First, they sort (u, q, s) triples by the predicted CTR and group them into buckets of similar predicted CTR values (1,000 triples in each bucket). Then, they compute the average predicted CTR x_i for triples in the i-th bucket as well as the average real CTR y_i for the same triples. The real CTR in this case equals the number of clicked triples divided by 1,000. Finally, they report the coefficient of determination R^2 between the vectors of simulated and real CTRs $\mathbf{x}$ and $\mathbf{y}$.

   A similar method was used by Xing et al. [2013] where ranks of the first and last clicks were used instead of CTRs. This method does not require any bucketing as click ranks can be

[3]Simulating clicks is also discussed below in Section 9.1.

computed for every session. As a measure, Xing et al. use mean absolute error (MAE), which is the average absolute difference between the real and predicted first/last click ranks.

The direct CTR estimation method discussed above removes limitations of the previous method by Chapelle and Zhang [2009]. In particular, it takes into account all documents, even the ones that never appear on the first position.

5.4 RELEVANCE PREDICTION EVALUATION

Click models are often used to predict relevance either directly or as a feature in a machine-learned ranking system. If a model operates with the notion of satisfaction (e.g., DCM, CCM and DBN),[4] the relevance of a document u with respect to a query q can be defined as follows:

$$R_{uq} = P(S_u = 1 \mid E_u = 1) = P(S_u = 1 \mid C_u = 1) \cdot P(C_u = 1 \mid E_u = 1) \qquad (5.9)$$

In the case of DBN (Section 3.8) this reduces to $R_{uq} = \sigma_{uq}\alpha_{uq}$. In the original DBN paper [Chapelle and Zhang, 2009] this notion of click model-based relevance has first been used verbatim as a ranking function and then tested as a feature in a machine learning-based ranking. The latter has also been used in [Dupret and Liao, 2010]. While the latter represents the more realistic situation of modern search engines (see, e.g., [Liu, 2009]), the former is preferable for reusable evaluation, since it depends neither on ranking features nor on the learning algorithm used. In both cases, a document ranking is evaluated using standard IR evaluation metrics such as DCG, NDCG [Järvelin and Kekäläinen, 2002] or AUC when only binary relevance labels are available.

One issue with this approach is that when underlying assumptions of an evaluation metric reflect those of a model, the model is going to get a high score, while this may not necessarily mean real quality improvements for the end user. As we will see in Section 9.4, one can build an evaluation metric from a user model and often the opposite is possible. In the latter case the model will receive high scores from the metric, but those might be artificial. To address this issue, Wang et al. [2015] suggest to compare metrics by showing two SERPs side by side to raters, where each SERP is ranked according to a particular click model. This evaluation method requires more rater resources, but allows one to circumvent the potential issues of IR evaluation metrics.

5.5 INTUITIVENESS EVALUATION FOR AGGREGATED SEARCH CLICK MODELS

Chuklin et al. [2014] propose an evaluation method for click models for aggregated search. *Aggregated search* (also referred to as *federated* search) is a type of search where results are retrieved from different *vertical* search engines (such as News, Sports or Video search engines) and then

---

[4]Even models that do not employ the notion of satisfaction can be useful in machine learning-based settings, where model parameters are used as ranking features.

presented in a special way on a SERP (see, e.g., [Arguello et al., 2009, 2012]). See Section 8.1 for more details.

Recently, a number of click models for aggregated search have been developed [Chen et al., 2012a, Chuklin et al., 2013b, Wang et al., 2013a]. While all the traditional evaluation methods are applicable to these vertical-aware models, it is sometimes important to look at the model performance on a more fine-grained level.

Zhou et al. [2013] explicitly name four components of aggregated search:

1. Vertical selection: which vertical search engines are relevant to a given query?

2. Item selection: which items should be selected from a given vertical?

3. Result presentation: how results from different verticals should be presented on a SERP.

4. Vertical diversity: how diverse the set of verticals should be.

Even if an aggregated system A is better than an aggregated system B overall, it may be important to know whether A loses to B in one of the above aspects. To evaluate this, a simple base metric was suggested for each aspect.

Chuklin et al. [2014] adapt this idea to evaluate click models for aggregated search. Similar to the above, four dimensions are used to show how well a particular click model can capture different aggregated search components. Multiple pairs of aggregated search systems are considered and the cases of disagreement where a click model assigns more clicks to the "worse" system (according to one of the four dimensions listed above) are counted. This is then repeated for different dimensions and different click models, and the click models are compared to each other by counting the amount of disagreement.

Now that we have discussed different evaluation methods for click models, we need only one more ingredient before we can evaluate the basic click models introduced in Chapter 3, viz. datasets and libraries, which are the topic of the next chapter.

CHAPTER 6

Data and Tools

To estimate parameters and evaluate the performance of click models, researchers use click logs, i.e., logs of user search sessions with click-through information (see page 7). Such logs are produced by live search systems and contain highly sensitive information in terms of privacy and commercial value. For this reason, publicly releasing such data while respecting privacy and the interests of the search engine owner is very challenging and requires a substantial amount of work. Still, substantial click logs have been available to academic researchers. In this chapter we discuss such publicly available click logs. We also describe software packages and libraries that we have found useful for working with click models.

6.1 DATASETS

One of the first publicly released datasets was the AOL query log released in 2006. It was a comprehensive dataset containing twenty million search sessions for over 650,000 users over a three-month period. The data was not redacted for privacy, which led the company to withdraw the dataset just a couple of days after its release.[1] It is one of the few datasets that contain actual queries and document URLs, which makes it valuable in spite of the fact that it represents a different generation of web search users interacting with a representative of a different generation of search engine. One of the drawbacks of this dataset is that it does not contain all documents shown to a user, only those that were clicked.

More recent releases include click logs from Microsoft[2] and Yandex,[3] published as part of the Web Search Click Data (WSCD) workshop series in 2009, 2012, 2013 and 2014. The WSCD 2009 dataset, also known as MSN 2006,[4] was collected from the MSN search engine in 2006 during a period of one month. The dataset contains query strings, grouped into sessions,[5] number of returned results and clicked URLs. The dataset cannot be downloaded directly, but is provided upon request.

The WSCD 2012 dataset[6] consists of user search sessions extracted from Yandex logs around 2009. The dataset contains anonymized queries, URL rankings, clicks and relevance judg-

---

[1]The dataset is still available for researchers through several mirrors.
[2]http://research.microsoft.com.
[3]http://yandex.com, the biggest search engine in Russia with significant presence in some other countries.
[4]http://research.microsoft.com/en-us/um/people/nickcr/wscd09/.
[5]Note that the notion of search session used in this dataset differs from our notion of query session (see Chapter 2).
[6]http://imat-relpred.yandex.ru/en/datasets.

Table 6.1: Summary of publicly available click log datasets

Dataset	Queries	URLs	Users	Sessions	Other Information
AOL 2006	10,154,742	1,632,788	657,426	21,011,340	Only clicked documents
MSN 2006	8,831,280	4,975,897	–	7,470,915	Only clicked documents
SogouQ 2012*	8,939,569	15,095,269	9,739,704	25,530,711	Only clicked documents
WSCD 2012	30,717,251	117,093,258	–	146,278,823	Judgements (71,930)
WSCD 2013	10,139,547	49,029,185	956,536	17,784,583	Search engine switches
WSCD 2014	21,073,569	70,348,426	5,736,333	65,172,853	Query terms, URL domains

* For SogouQ the number of unique query-user pairs is reported instead of the session count; the actual number of sessions may be higher.

ments for ranked URLs. In addition, queries are grouped into search sessions. We use this dataset for our experiments in Chapter 7.

The WSCD 2013 dataset[7] [Serdyukov et al., 2013] was extracted from Yandex logs around 2011. In addition to information provided by WSCD 2012, this dataset contains anonymized user ids and search engine switching actions (i.e., indicators that a user switched from Yandex to other search engines during a search session). The WSCD 2013 dataset does not contain relevance judgements.

The WSCD 2014 dataset[8] [Serdyukov et al., 2014], collected around 2012 over a period of one month, contains personalized rankings for more than five million users. Compared to WSCD 2012, this dataset also provides query terms and domains of ranked URLs, but does not provide relevance judgements.

Sogou[9] also released two click log datasets, called SogouQ.[10] The first dataset was released in 2008; in 2012 it was replaced by a bigger dataset. Similarly to the WSCD datasets, SogouQ contains anonymized user ids, queries, URL rankings and clicks. Unlike the Yandex datasets, however, query strings and document URLs are not obfuscated and provided verbatim in the click log. This allows researchers to perform query similarity analysis, document analysis and other applications that are not possible with numeric ids. The downside of this dataset is that it only provides information about clicked documents, so the exact set of documents shown to a user can only be approximated.

The statistics of publicly available click logs is given in Table 6.1. Although these logs largely facilitate research on click models for web search, they are limited to the standard results presentation paradigm (known as "ten blue links") and to searches performed on desktop computers. As we show in Chapter 8, current developments of click models go beyond these limitations and consider user search intents, results of vertical search engines (e.g., Image or News search engines) and even other types of user interaction, such as eye-gaze and mouse movements. Unfortunately,

---

[7]http://switchdetect.yandex.ru/en.

[8]https://www.kaggle.com/c/yandex-personalized-web-search-challenge.

[9]http://www.sogou.com, one of the biggest search engines in China.

[10]http://www.sogou.com/labs/dl/q-e.html; as of 2015 the files are encoded using the GB18030 character set, not UTF-8.

at the time of writing there are still no publicly available datasets suitable for working with these advanced click models.

In this context, it is worth mentioning ad datasets published by Criteo.[11] The 2014[12] and 2015[13] releases contain ads served by Criteo (represented using 39 integer features) and click events. The Criteo datasets are not directly suitable for training and testing click models for web search, but could be used to experiment with domain-specific models (e.g., click models for ads [Yin et al., 2014]).

6.2   SOFTWARE TOOLS AND OPEN SOURCE PROJECTS

A number of software tools and libraries are suitable for working with click models: from dedicated projects like ClickModels[14] and PyClick,[15] through more general tools like Infer.NET[16] and Lerot,[17] to general-purpose languages such as Octave[18] or Matlab.[19]

The ClickModels project, written in Python, provides an open source implementation of state-of-the-art click models, namely the dynamic Bayesian network model (DBN) [Chapelle and Zhang, 2009] (simplified and full versions), the dependent click model (DCM) [Guo et al., 2009b] and the user browsing model (UBM) [Dupret and Piwowarski, 2008]. It also implements the exploration bias extension of UBM according to Chen et al. [2012a]. A special feature of this project is the implementation of intent-aware extensions of the above models according to Chuklin et al. [2013b]. Overall, the ClickModels project is suitable for training and testing standard click models for web search as well as advanced models that consider user search intents.

The PyClick open source project, also written in Python, aims to provide an extendable implementation of existing click models and to simplify the development of new models. PyClick implements all basic click models discussed in Chapter 3. It mainly uses standard parameter estimation techniques described in Chapter 4, i.e., maximum likelihood estimation (MLE) and expectation-maximization (EM). In addition, it implements two alternative parameter estimation techniques, namely probit Bayesian inference (PBI) [Zhang et al., 2010] and the Bayesian browsing model (BBM) [Liu et al., 2009]. PyClick can also be used as a basis for the rapid development of new click models. We use PyClick to perform experiments in Chapter 7.

Infer.NET, created and maintained by Microsoft Research, is a framework for running Bayesian inference in graphical models. It is fast, scalable and well-supported. Infer.NET provides algorithms to solve various machine learning problems and, in particular, can be used to train click models. The advantage of this framework is that it can be used for a wide range of tasks beyond

---

[11]http://www.criteo.com.
[12]https://www.kaggle.com/c/criteo-display-ad-challenge.
[13]http://labs.criteo.com/2015/03/criteo-releases-its-new-dataset.
[14]https://github.com/varepsilon/clickmodels.
[15]https://github.com/markovi/PyClick.
[16]http://research.microsoft.com/en-us/um/cambridge/projects/infernet.
[17]https://bitbucket.org/ilps/lerot.
[18]https://www.gnu.org/software/octave.
[19]http://mathworks.com/products/matlab.

click models. On the other hand, Infer.NET is limited to non-commercial use and does not provide out-of-the-box implementations of existing click models.

The Lerot project [Schuth et al., 2013], implemented in Python, is designed to run experiments with online learning to rank methods. Lerot uses click models to simulate user clicks and, for this purpose, implements some basic models, such as the random click model (RCM), the position-based model (PBM) and the cascade model (CM) (see Chapter 3). It is also integrated with the ClickModels project, so that a wider range of click models can be used for simulation within Lerot.

Finally, general-purpose languages, such as Octave and Matlab, provide a number of ready-to-use inference and evaluation methods, which can be used to implement click models. These languages are highly flexible, but of course do not provide any specific support for click models.

In summary, existing software tools and open source projects implement many of the click models proposed in the literature so far and support the development of new models. When working with click models, researchers and practitioners have access to a solid set of tools ranging from highly specific projects with many implemented models but relatively low flexibility to general-purpose languages with high flexibility but no out-of-the-box implementations.

CHAPTER 7

Experimental Comparison

Existing studies of click models usually evaluate only a subset of available click models, often use proprietary data, rely on different evaluation metrics and rarely publish the source code used to produce the results. This makes it hard to compare the reported results between different studies. In this chapter, we present a comprehensive evaluation of the click models described in Chapter 3 using a publicly available dataset (see Chapter 6), an open-source implementation (again, see Chapter 6) and a set of commonly used evaluation metrics (see Chapter 5).

7.1   EXPERIMENTAL SETUP

We use the WSCD 2012 dataset discussed in Section 6.1 (see Table 6.1 for more statistics). More specifically, we use the first one million sessions of the dataset to train and test the basic click models.[1] We train models on the first 75% of the sessions and test them on the last 25%. This is done to simulate the real-world application where the model is trained using historical data and applied to unseen future sessions. Since sessions in the dataset are grouped by user tasks, we are not fully guaranteed to have a strict chronological ordering between training and test material, but this is the closest we can get. Since the basic click models introduced in Chapter 3 cannot handle unseen query-document pairs, we filter the test set to contain only queries that appear in the training set. The statistics of the training and test sets are given in Table 7.1.

In order to verify that the results hold for other subsets of the data and to report confidence intervals for our results, we repeat our experiment 15 times, each time selecting the next million sessions from the dataset and creating the same training-test split as described above. We then report the 95% confidence intervals using the bootstrap method [Efron and Tibshirani, 1994].

All click models are implemented in Python within the PyClick library described in Section 6.2. The expectation maximization algorithm (EM) uses 50 iterations. The DCM model is implemented in its simplified form (SDCM) according to the original study [Guo et al., 2009b] (see Section 4.1.2). To measure the quality of click models, we use log-likelihood and perplexity, both the standard and conditional versions, which are the most commonly used evaluation metrics for click models. In addition, we report the time it took us to train each model using a single CPU core[2] and the PyPy interpreter.[3]

---

[1]We also experimented with ten million sessions and the results were qualitatively similar to what we present here.
[2]Intel® Xeon® CPU E5-2650 0 @ 2.00 GHz, 20 MB L2 cache.
[3]http://pypy.org.

Table 7.1: Statistics of the training and test sets

Set	# Sessions	# Unique Queries
Training	750,000	322,799
Test	139,009	23,465

Table 7.2: Log-likelihood, perplexity, conditional perplexity and training time of basic click models for web search as calculated on the first one million sessions of the WSCD 2012 dataset. The best values for each metric are indicated in boldface.

Model	Log-likelihood	Perplexity	Cond. perplexity	Time (sec)
RCM	−0.3727	1.5325	1.5325	**2.37**
RCTR	−0.3017	1.3730	1.3730	2.45
DCTR	−0.3082	1.3713	1.3713	9.39
PBM	−0.2757	1.3323	1.3323	77.95
CM	−∞	1.3675	+∞	12.17
UBM	**−0.2568**	1.3321	**1.3093**	113.53
SDCM	−0.2974	1.3315	1.3588	15.53
CCM	−0.2807	1.3406	1.3412	2,993.03
DBN	−0.2680	1.3311	1.3217	1,661.16
SDBN	−0.2940	**1.3270**	1.3538	17.42

7.2   RESULTS AND DISCUSSION

The results of our experimental comparison are shown in Table 7.2. The table reports log-likelihood, perplexity, conditional perplexity and training time. The best values for each evaluation metric are indicated in boldface. Below we discuss the results for each metric.

Log-likelihood.   The log-likelihood metric shows how well a model approximates the observed data. In our case, it shows how well a click model approximates observed user clicks in a set of query sessions (see Section 5.1). Table 7.2 and Figure 7.1 report the log-likelihood values for all basic click models. Notice that the cascade model (CM) cannot handle query sessions with more than one click and gives zero probabilities to all clicks below the first one. For such sessions, the log-likelihood of CM is $\log 0 = -\infty$ and, thus, the total log-likelihood of CM is $-\infty$. Similarly, the value of conditional perplexity for CM is $2^{-\log 0} = +\infty$. Notice that we could consider only sessions with one click to evaluate the CM model. However, this would make the CM log-likelihood values incomparable to those of other click models.

Since most click models have the same set of attractiveness parameters that depend on queries and documents (apart from RCM and DCTR), the main difference between the models is the way they treat examination parameters (e.g., the number of examination parameters and

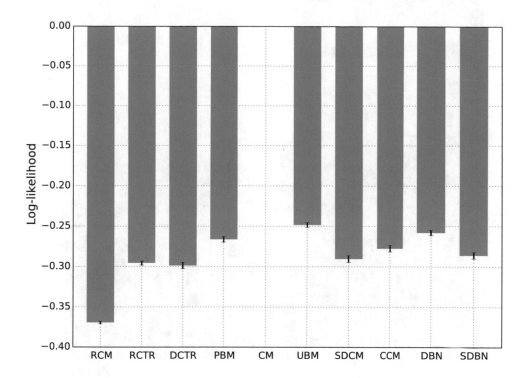

Figure 7.1: Log-likelihood values for different models; higher is better. Error bars correspond to the 95% bootstrap confidence intervals. The cascade model (CM) is excluded because it cannot handle multiple clicks in a session.

the estimation technique).[4] Thus, it is natural to expect that models with more examination parameters, which are estimated in connection to other parameters (i.e., using the EM algorithm), should better approximate observed data.

The results in Table 7.2 and Figure 7.1 generally confirm this intuition. UBM, having the largest number of examination parameters, which are estimated using EM, appears to be the best model in terms of approximating user clicks based on previous clicks and skips. It is followed by DBN (one examination parameter, a set of satisfaction parameters, EM algorithm) and PBM (ten examination parameters, EM algorithm). Other models have noticeably lower log-likelihood with the RCM baseline being significantly worse than the others as expected.

Notice that DBN outperforms PBM and SDBN outperforms SDCM (although not significantly), respectively, having fewer examination parameters and using the same estimation technique. This is due to the fact that DBN and SDBN have a large set of satisfaction parameters that

---

[4]Notice that DBN and SDBN differ from other models also by considering satisfaction parameters that depend on queries and documents.

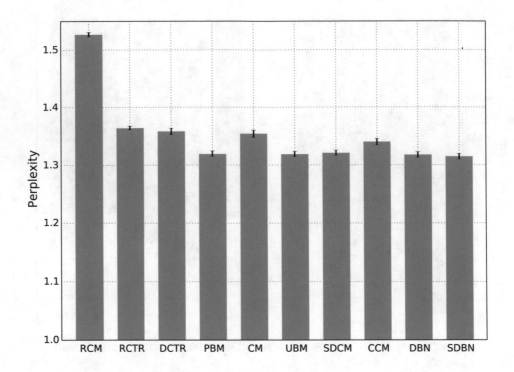

Figure 7.2: Perplexity values for different models; lower is better. Error bars correspond to the 95% bootstrap confidence intervals.

also affect examination. Overall, the above results show that complex models are able to describe user clicks better than the simple CTR models, which confirms the usefulness of these models.

As expected, simple models, namely RCTR, DCTR and RCM, have the lowest log-likelihood. Notice, however, that RCTR and DCTR do not differ much from SDCM and SDBN, while being much simpler and sometimes much faster (RCTR). Still, the downside of these simple CTR-based models is that they do not explain user behavior on a SERP, as opposed to SDCM and SDBN that explicitly define examination and click behavior and that can, therefore, be used in a number of applications of click models (see Chapter 9).

Perplexity.   Perplexity shows how well a click model can predict user clicks in a query session when previous clicks and skips in that session are not known (the lower the better). Table 7.2 shows that this version of perplexity (defined in Section 5.2) does not directly correlate with log-likelihood. Therefore, we believe that the standard perplexity should be preferred over the conditional perplexity for the task of click model evaluation because it gives a different perspective compared to log-likelihood.

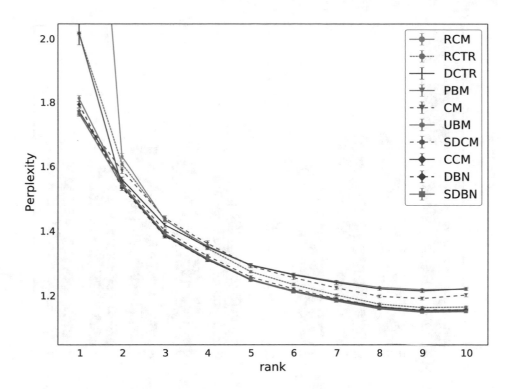

Figure 7.3: Perplexity values for different models and at different ranks; lower is better. Error bars correspond to the 95% bootstrap confidence intervals.

When ranking click models based on the perplexity values (see Table 7.2 and Figures 7.2 and 7.3) the best model is SDBN followed by DBN, SDCM, UBM and PBM, respectively. The results show that complex click models perform better than CTR not only in terms of log-likelihood but also in terms of perplexity.

By looking at perplexity values for different ranks, as shown in Figure 7.3, one can see that, apart from the simple CTR-based models and the cascade model, all the models show similar perplexity results with the biggest difference observed for rank 1.

Conditional perplexity.   As discussed in Section 5.2.1, conditional perplexity can be seen as a per rank decomposition of the likelihood. Indeed, Table 7.2 and Figure 7.4 show that the conditional perplexity produces the same ranking of click models as log-likelihood (apart from RCTR and DCTR, whose ranks are swapped). This means that conditional perplexity does not add much additional information when used together with log-likelihood for click model evaluation.

By looking at a per-rank decomposition (Figure 7.5) one can see a more non-trivial pattern. First, UBM is a clear leader starting from rank 4, suggesting that knowing the distance to the last

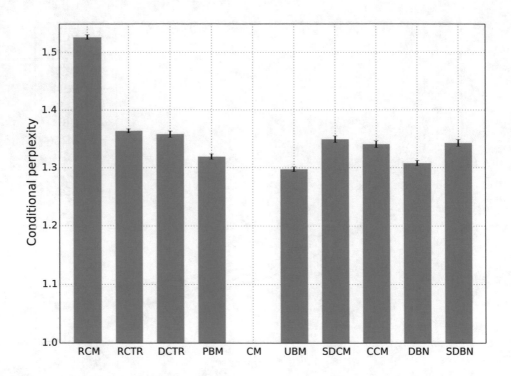

Figure 7.4: Conditional perplexity values for different models; lower is better. Error bars correspond to the 95% bootstrap confidence intervals. Cascade Model (CM) is excluded because it cannot handle multiple clicks in a session.

click is quite useful for the examination prediction (cf. Section 3.5). DBN also shows quite good results for higher ranks, much better than SDBN, although not as good as UBM. Surprisingly, predicting a click on the first position is easier for SDBN than for the more complex DBN model. This suggests that the DBN assumptions work either for higher ranks or for lower ranks (with different γ parameter values), but cannot quite explain user behavior as a whole.

Training time.   The amount of time required to train a click model (Figure 7.6) directly relates to the estimation method used. The maximum-likelihood estimation (MLE) iterates through training sessions only once and, thus, it is much faster than EM, which uses a large number of iterations. Click models estimated using MLE require from two to 18 seconds to train on 750,000 query sessions, where the fastest models are RCM and RCTR. The EM-based models, instead, require from one to 50 minutes to be trained on the same number of sessions, where the slowest model is CCM. In fact, CCM is over 60% slower than DBN, which, in turn, is over ten times slower than any other model studied here.

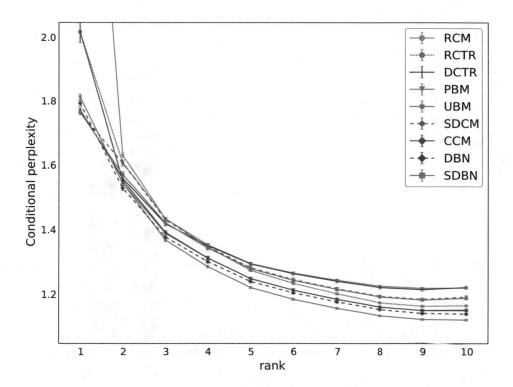

Figure 7.5: Conditional perplexity values for different models and at different ranks; lower is better. Error bars correspond to the 95% bootstrap confidence intervals. The cascade model (CM) is excluded because it cannot handle multiple clicks in a session.

One of the things to mention here is that the choice of PyPy as a Python interpreter was crucial. Just this simple switch reduced the training time of DBN from 39 hours to 28 minutes; similar dramatic drops were observed for all other models.

7.3   SUMMARY

In this chapter we have provided a comparison of the basic click models introduced in Chapter 3, using two core evaluation metrics, namely log-likelihood and perplexity. While we include all the basic models in our analysis, there are many dimensions that we did not look at, such as prediction of clicks vs. prediction of their absence, query frequency and query entropy analysis, to name a few. For those additional dimensions, we refer the reader to a complementary study by Grotov et al. [2015].

Overall, complex click models, namely PBM, UBM, SDCM, CCM, DBN and SDBN, outperform CTR-based models and the cascade model both in terms of log-likelihood and per-

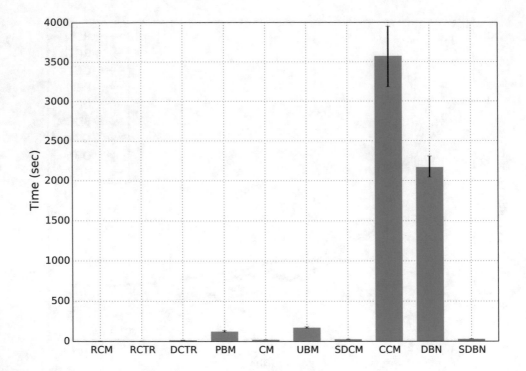

Figure 7.6: Training time for different click models; lower is better.

plexity. Also, the models whose parameters are estimated using the EM algorithm (PBM, UBM, CCM and DBN) tend to outperform those estimated using the MLE technique (SDCM and SDBN), because in the former case model parameters are estimated in connection to each other. However, such models take much longer to train.

When comparing pairs of more complex and simplified models (DBN/SDBN and CCM/SDCM) one can see that the simplified one yields better perplexity values but worse conditional perplexity and likelihood scores. We believe that these simplifications together with the MLE algorithm can find more robust estimations for the model parameters, but cannot fully interpret the relation between past and future behavior in the same session.

There is no clear winner among the best performing models, but UBM tends to have the highest log-likelihood and almost the lowest perplexity. A potential drawback of UBM, however, is that the interpretation of its examination parameters is not straightforward (see Section 3.5). UBM is closely followed by DBN and PBM, which sometimes have slightly worse performance, but their parameters are easier to interpret.

CHAPTER 8

Advanced Click Models

In this chapter we summarize more recent click models that somehow improve over the basic click models studied in Chapter 3. Most of these models build on one of the basic click models by introducing new parameters, using more data and, more generally, incorporating additional knowledge about user behavior.

We start by describing click models for aggregated search in Section 8.1. In Section 8.2 we discuss models that aim to predict user behavior that spans across multiple query sessions. Section 8.3 is devoted to models that exploit user diversity at different granularity levels. In Section 8.4 we talk about models that use additional signals such as mouse or eye movements, while in Section 8.5 we talk about models that make use of relevance labels. In Section 8.6 we discuss models that capture non-linearity in user examination behavior. And finally, in Section 8.7, we briefly discuss models that make use of feature-based machine learning in addition to a probabilistic modeling framework.

8.1 AGGREGATED SEARCH

In this section we discuss click models for aggregated search. As explained in Section 5.5, *aggregated search* (also known as *federated search*) is a search paradigm where a SERP *aggregates* results from multiple sources known as *verticals* (e.g., News, Image or Video verticals). All major web search engines have adopted this mode of presentation by adding blocks of vertical results to their SERPs; see Figure 8.1 for an example.

8.1.1 FEDERATED CLICK MODEL (FCM)

It is evident from Figure 8.1 that vertical blocks on an aggregated SERP can be more visually salient and attract more user attention than other results on the SERP. Moreover, Chen et al. [2012a] show that vertical blocks also affect the amount of attention that nearby non-vertical documents get. For example, if there is an image vertical placed at rank 4, then the chance of the document at rank 3 being clicked is more than twice as high as normal. To account for this, Chen et al. introduce a parameter called "attention bias" A, which is a binary variable.[1] If A equals 1, then documents near vertical blocks have a higher chance of being examined:

$$P(A = 1) = \chi_c \qquad (8.1)$$
$$P(E_r = 1 \mid A = 0, \mathbf{E}_{<r}, \mathbf{S}_{<r}, \mathbf{C}_{<r}) = \epsilon_r \qquad (8.2)$$

---

[1]Not to be confused with the attractiveness variable A_u which always has a subscript.

Figure 8.1: An example of a search engine result page featuring organic results as well as results from Image and Video verticals for the query "Amsterdam."

$$P(E_r = 1 \mid A = 1, \mathbf{E}_{<r}, \mathbf{S}_{<r}, \mathbf{C}_{<r}) = \epsilon_r + (1 - \epsilon_r)\beta_{dist}, \tag{8.3}$$

where the parameter β is indexed by the distance from the current document u to the nearest vertical block $vert$, i.e., $dist = r_u - r_{vert}$ ($dist$ can be negative); ϵ_r is the examination probability in the absence of vertical attention bias. The parameter χ_c can either depend on the position of a vertical block (i.e., $\chi_{r_{vert}}$) or on the content of the block (i.e., χ_{vert}).

Notice that through the parameter ϵ_r different click models can be extended to a vertical-aware model (called FCM for *federated click model* in [Chen et al., 2012a]). For example, UBM (Section 3.5) can be extended to FCM-UBM as follows:

$$P(A = 1) = \chi_c \tag{8.4}$$
$$P(E_r = 1 \mid A = 0, \mathbf{C}_{<\mathbf{r}}) = \gamma_{rr'} \tag{8.5}$$
$$P(E_r = 1 \mid A = 1, \mathbf{C}_{<\mathbf{r}}) = \gamma_{rr'} + (1 - \gamma_{rr'})\beta_{dist}. \tag{8.6}$$

The FCM model has been extended to take into account the fact that some users may have a stronger bias to a particular vertical and tend to skip organic web results [Chen et al., 2012a]. Later, it has also been extended to account for multiple verticals [Chuklin et al., 2014, 2015].

8.1.2   VERTICAL CLICK MODEL (VCM)

After performing a thorough analysis of different peculiarities related to verticals, Wang et al. [2013a] suggest a complex model that is based on UBM (Section 3.5) and incorporates four types of bias:

1. **Attraction bias.** If there is a vertical on a SERP, there is a certain probability that a user starts examining the SERP from this vertical.

2. **Global bias.** If the user starts examining the SERP from the vertical result, this affects their further behavior (both the examination and attractiveness probabilities change).

3. **First place bias.** If there is a vertical on the first position, it affects further behavior of the user. This is a special case of the global bias.

4. **Sequence bias.** If the user starts examining the SERP from the vertical block, they may continue examining documents from top to bottom, or first examine documents above the vertical in reversed order and only then proceed in the normal top-to-bottom order.

Wang et al. perform a detailed eye-tracking and click log analysis to study these biases and show that a click model incorporating all of them outperforms UBM in both perplexity and log-likelihood. The detailed description of the model can be found in the original paper [Wang et al., 2013a].

8.1.3   INTENT-AWARE CLICK MODELS

Chuklin et al. [2013b] suggest to look at aggregated search as if there are different users coming with different intents (needs): organic web, Image, News, Video, etc. If we assume that these intents are independent, than the click probability decomposes as follows:

$$P(C_1, \ldots, C_n) = \sum_i P(I = i) \cdot P(C_1, \ldots, C_n \mid I = i), \qquad (8.7)$$

where $P(I = i)$ is the probability of the i-th intent. One may then use different examination and click probabilities for different intents, assuming that the intent distribution $P(I = i)$ is known for each query.

The authors suggest to go one step further and also take visual aspects into account, hypothesizing that the use of special presentation formats, e.g., News results enhanced with a thumbnail, will lead to different examination patterns than if these results are presented as organic web results.

For example, the intent-aware version of UBM (Section 3.5), UBM-IA, can be written as follows:

$$P(E_r = 1 \mid G_r = b, I = i, \mathbf{C}_{<\mathbf{r}}) = \gamma_{rr'}(b, i) \qquad (8.8)$$
$$P(C_r = 1 \mid I = i, E_r = 1) = \alpha^i_{u_r q}, \qquad (8.9)$$

where G_r is the presentation type of a document at rank r (e.g., standard snippet, thumbnail-enhanced news, etc.). In the simplest case both I and G_r random variables take two possible values: organic web or vertical.

One nice bonus of the intent-aware extension is that it can be applied on top of any model, including the FCM model discussed above [Chen et al., 2012a]. The resulting model outperforms the original FCM model in terms of perplexity [Chuklin et al., 2013b].

8.2   BEYOND A SINGLE QUERY SESSION

8.2.1   PAGINATION

Modern SERPs usually contain roughly ten results, but a user can request more results by clicking on pagination buttons. As reported in [Chuklin et al., 2013d], each session has a click on a pagination button with a probability of 5–10%. The new set of documents available after the pagination action obviously should not be treated as a new session, but it cannot be viewed as a simple continuation of the previous page either. Chuklin et al. [2013d] show that by explicitly adding pagination buttons as a clickable SERP object into a click model one can substantially improve over a baseline model, which, in this case, works as if a user would see an infinite list of documents at once without the need to click on pagination buttons. Two models based on DBN (Section 3.8) are proposed in which the click and examination probabilities of the pagination button may or may not depend on a query. The authors show that both extensions outperform the baseline DBN model after the first result page with one or another model giving better perplexity at different rank positions.

8.2.2   TASK-CENTRIC CLICK MODEL (TCM)

Zhang et al. [2011] present a general notion of a search task, where two consecutive query sessions do not necessarily share the same query (as opposed to the case of pagination discussed in the previous section) but rather represent the same task from the user's perspective, such as, e.g., buying a concert ticket.[2] After performing a qualitative analysis, the authors formulate two assumptions about sessions in a task:

1. **Query bias.** If a query does not match the user's information need, the results are not clicked and the query is reformulated based on the presented results to better match the information need.

2. **Duplicate bias.** If the same document appears again in the same task, it has a lower probability of being clicked.

Zhang et al. formalize this within the task-centric click model (TCM):

$$P(M = 1) = \tau_1 \tag{8.10}$$

$$P(N = 1 \mid M = 0) = 1 \tag{8.11}$$

$$P(N = 1 \mid M = 1) = \tau_2 \tag{8.12}$$

$$P(H_r = 1 \mid H_{r'}^{s'} = 0, E_{r'}^{s'} = 0) = 0 \tag{8.13}$$

$$P(F_r = 1 \mid H_r = 0) = 1 \tag{8.14}$$

$$P(F_r = 1 \mid H_r = 1) = \tau_3 \tag{8.15}$$

$$P(E_r = 1 \mid \mathbf{E}_{<r}, \mathbf{S}_{<r}, \mathbf{C}_{<r}) = \epsilon_r \tag{8.16}$$

[2]In practice, users may switch between several tasks while browsing (a phenomenon called *multitasking*). In that case, sessions that belong to the same task do not have to be consecutive.

$$P(A_r = 1) = \alpha_{u_r q} \tag{8.17}$$
$$C_r = 1 \Leftrightarrow M = 1, F_r = 1, E_r = 1 \text{ and } A_r = 1. \tag{8.18}$$

The notation should be read as follows:

- M: whether a session matches a user need;

- N: whether a user is going to submit another query in the same task;

- H_r: whether the document u_r occurred in some earlier session; if so, its previous occurrence was in a session s' at rank r';

- F_r: whether the document u_r is considered "fresh";

- E_r: examination (see Chapter 2);

- A_r: attractiveness (see Chapter 2);

- C_r: click (see Chapter 2);

The TCM model can be built on top of any basic click model (Chapter 3). This basic click model determines the parameters α_{uq} and ϵ_r. Zhang et al. show that the TCM models built on top of DBN and UBM outperform the corresponding basic models in terms of perplexity (Section 5.2) and relevance prediction (Section 5.4).

8.3   USER AND QUERY DIVERSITY

It is well-known that there is a certain variability between different users and different sessions [White and Drucker, 2007]. One user may be very persistent and click many results while another may just abandon a SERP without spending much effort. Over time, different approaches to capture user diversity have been developed: from considering session variability and query variability to directly incorporating users into click models. In the next sections we describe the corresponding click models.

8.3.1   SESSION VARIABILITY

Hu et al. [2011] are the first to formally introduce user diversity in a click model. They start with the idea that different users come to a search box with different notions of relevance and some users may decide not to click a document even if it looks attractive overall. For this purpose they introduce a session-dependent parameter μ_s that decreases the attractiveness probability:

$$P(A_u = 1) = P(C_u = 1 \mid E_u = 1) = \mu_s a_{uq}. \tag{8.19}$$

The authors build corresponding click models based on UBM and DBN (calling them Unbiased-UBM and Unbiased-DBN, respectively), each one outperforming the corresponding basic model in terms of log-likelihood (Section 5.1) and relevance prediction (Section 5.4).

8.3.2 QUERY VARIABILITY

Varying persistence (DBN-VP).   Ashkan and Clarke [2012] suggest to make model parameters query-dependent, which is especially useful in the context of commercial search where different queries have different levels of commercial intent and hence different user persistence in clicking links. They apply this idea to the DBN model (Section 3.8) by modifying (3.40) and replacing it with the following:

$$P(E_r = 1 \mid E_{r-1} = 1, S_{r-1} = 0) = \gamma_q, \tag{8.20}$$

where the user perseverance γ_q now depends on a query. They call this model DBN-VP (varying persistence) and show that it outperforms the baseline DBN for commercial search in terms of log-likelihood and perplexity.

A similar but simpler idea is used by Guo et al. [2009a]. They suggest to train the CCM model (Section 3.7) for navigational and informational queries separately, which results in substantially different persistence parameters τ_i for different query classes.

Intent-aware models.   The idea of query-dependent parameters is similar to the intent-aware models by Chuklin et al. [2013b] considered above. Instead of having model parameters directly depend on a query, Chuklin et al. assume a smaller set of user intents. The intents do not have to correspond to verticals as discussed above. Instead, they can be used to differentiate users with different goals. For example, we can introduce the following intents: "searching definition," "fact checking" or "entertainment." These intents will have different perseverance parameters in the case of intent-aware DBN (DBN-intents model in [Chuklin et al., 2013b]):

$$P(E_r = 1 \mid I = i, E_{r-1} = 1, S_{r-1} = 0) = \gamma(i). \tag{8.21}$$

Each query will then have an intent distribution $P(I = i)$ and the final click probability can be obtained by marginalizing over this distribution.

8.3.3 USER VARIABILITY

Matrix factorization click model (MFCM).   Shen et al. [2012] are the first to formally incorporate users into click models. In order to do so, they say that the attractiveness parameter $\alpha_{uq} = P(A_u = 1)$ has a Gaussian prior that depends on the document matrix U_u, the query matrix Q_q and the user matrix V_v:

$$P(A_u = 1) = \alpha_{uqv} \tag{8.22}$$
$$P(\alpha_{uqv} \mid U_u, Q_q, V_v, \sigma) \sim \mathcal{N}\left((U_u \circ Q_q \circ V_v), \sigma^2\right) \tag{8.23}$$
$$P(U_u \mid \sigma_u) \sim \mathcal{N}(0, \sigma_u^2) \tag{8.24}$$
$$P(Q_q \mid \sigma_q) \sim \mathcal{N}(0, \sigma_q^2) \tag{8.25}$$
$$P(V_v \mid \sigma_v) \sim \mathcal{N}(0, \sigma_v^2), \tag{8.26}$$

where $U_u \circ Q_q \circ V_v = \sum_f U_{fu} Q_{fq} V_{fv}$ is a tensor factorization. While this personalized click model (PCM) directly adds a user component to the model, it may have overfitting issues for cases where user differences are not important, for instance, navigational queries. In order to solve this problem, the authors suggest a so-called *hybrid personalized click model* (HPCM) where a non-personalized component is added to the personalized one:

$$P(\alpha_{uqv} \mid U_u, Q_q, V_v, \sigma) \sim \mathcal{N}\left((\tilde{U}_u \circ \tilde{Q}_q + U_u \circ Q_q \circ V_v), \sigma^2\right). \tag{8.27}$$

Each matrix above has its own Gaussian prior similar to the earlier case of PCM.

Experiments show that the HPCM model (based on UBM) consistently outperforms all other models in terms of both log-likelihood and perplexity and hence represents a good trade-off between the fully personalized and regular click model that treats users homogeneously.

Incorporating users.   Xing et al. [2013] take a more direct approach and simply add a user-based parameter into a click model:

$$P(A_u = 1) = \alpha_{uq}\epsilon_v, \tag{8.28}$$

where v denotes a user.

The above model, called UBM-user and based on UBM (Section 3.5), already gives a small improvement over the baseline model in terms of perplexity and CTR prediction. A few other modifications are suggested, two of which perform exceptionally well, with over 10% perplexity gain (5.6) on the test set; both modifications are based on UBM.

The first of these two modifications is a *logistic model* (LOG-rd-user), which modifies the examination and attractiveness probabilities separately:

$$P(E_r = 1 \mid \mathbf{C}_{<\mathbf{r}}) = \sigma\left(\gamma_{rr'} + \varepsilon_v\right) \tag{8.29}$$
$$P(A_r = 1) = \sigma\left(\alpha_{u_r q} + \epsilon_v\right), \tag{8.30}$$

where ε_v and ϵ_v are the two user-dependent parameters and $\sigma(x) = 1/(1 + \exp(-x))$ is a logistic function (sigmoid). Here, the α and γ parameters do not have to lie between 0 and 1 as this is guaranteed by the logistic transformation.

Another modification, called the *dilution model* (DIL-user), is specifically designed to mitigate the risk of overfitting. This is done by simplifying the UBM examination probability parameter $\gamma_{rr'}$ and splitting it into the term that depends on the rank r and the term that depends on the distance to the previous click $r - r'$:

$$P(E_r = 1 \mid \mathbf{C}_{<\mathbf{r}}) = (\beta_v)^{r-1}(\lambda_v)^k(\mu_v)^{r-r'} \tag{8.31}$$
$$P(A_r = 1) = \alpha_{u_r q}\epsilon_v, \tag{8.32}$$

where k is the total number of clicks before r and β_v, λ_v and μ_v are the three user-dependent dumping factors, which control how the examination probability diminishes with increasing rank, increasing number of previous clicks and the distance to the previous click, respectively.

8.4　EYE TRACKING AND MOUSE MOVEMENTS

Since the work of Huang et al. [2011] it has become clear that mouse movement data can be collected at scale. With almost no additional resources, exact coordinates of a mouse cursor can be stored in a search log on top of the click events data. As has been shown in multiple experiments [Chen et al., 2001, Rodden et al., 2008], mouse movements can serve as a robust proxy to result examination and can help to estimate the examination probability.

Mousing and scrolling as hints to examination.　Huang et al. [2012] suggest to use mouse movements and page scrolls as additional data that helps to detect examination events E that are not observed directly. The authors suggest a refined DBN model that benefits from this additional source of data by adding the following constraints:

$$P(E_r = 1 \mid \exists h \in H : r \leq r_h) = 1 \tag{8.33}$$
$$P(E_r = 1 \mid r \in V) = 1, \tag{8.34}$$

where H is the set of hovered documents (mousing) and V is the set of all documents shown when a user scrolled a SERP (scrolling). Results show that augmenting the model with this additional data leads to improved perplexity.

From skimming to reading.　Recent work by Liu et al. [2014] suggests that mouse movements themselves or even eye positions obtained with an eye tracker do not necessarily indicate that a user is reading a snippet. Instead, two separate states should be considered: skimming a document and reading a document:

$$P(C_u = 1) = P(C_u = 1 \mid R_u = 1) \cdot P(R_u = 1 \mid F_u = 1) \cdot P(F_u = 1), \tag{8.35}$$

where R_u is an additional random variable corresponding to *reading* the document u as opposed to skimming or fixing eyes on u, i.e., F_u. The authors show that training separate models for each of the factors above yields better relevance prediction (Section 5.4).

Predicting mousing instead of clicks.　Diaz et al. [2013] take the first steps toward modeling mouse movements themselves. They suggest a Markov model that predicts the probability of mousing element j after element i. While in most of the click models studied above it is assumed that documents are examined from top to bottom, the order may be different when a result page is non-linear. For instance, the result page of an image search engine typically contains results in the form of a grid and the top-to-bottom examination assumption is simply not applicable in this case.

　　　Diaz et al. demonstrate that complex sequences of mouse movements can be predicted reasonably well and that their model can generalize to unseen SERP layouts.

8.5   USING EDITORIAL RELEVANCE JUDGEMENTS

As we discussed in Section 6.1, there is a very limited amount of publicly available click data and each of the public datasets has its own drawbacks. On the other hand, there are multiple datasets available, which contain rankings produced by different search systems and relevance labels obtained from judges. This includes, but is not limited to, the TREC datasets [Voorhees and Harman, 2001], the Microsoft LETOR datasets [Liu et al., 2007], the Yahoo! Learning to Rank Challenge[3] and the Yandex Internet Mathematics Challenge.[4] Below we discuss different approaches to incorporating relevance judgements into click models, which benefit from datasets that come with relevance judgements.

Using only editorial relevance.   Hofmann et al. [2011] suggest to instantiate click model parameters based on editorial relevance judgements. As has been shown by Turpin et al. [2009], attractiveness parameters α_{uq} appearing in most of the models are reasonably well correlated with editorial relevance judgements R_{uq}. The same holds for satisfaction parameters σ_{uq} appearing in DBN or in any model with the notion of satisfaction. This allows us to greatly reduce the number of click model parameters by making the assumption that any parameter θ_{uq} is a function of the relevance judgement R_{uq}. This means that instead of having a separate parameter value for every query-document pair, we only need to have one value for each relevance grade. For example, the DBN model can then be specified as follows (cf. (3.34)–(3.40)):

$$C_r = 1 \Leftrightarrow E_r = 1 \text{ and } A_r = 1 \tag{8.36}$$
$$P(A_r = 1) = \alpha(R_{u_r q}) \tag{8.37}$$
$$P(E_1 = 1) = 1 \tag{8.38}$$
$$P(E_r = 1 \mid E_{r-1} = 0) = 0 \tag{8.39}$$
$$P(S_r = 1 \mid C_r = 1) = \sigma(R_{u_r q}) \tag{8.40}$$
$$P(E_r = 1 \mid S_{r-1} = 1) = 0 \tag{8.41}$$
$$P(E_r = 1 \mid E_{r-1} = 1, S_{r-1} = 0) = \gamma. \tag{8.42}$$

If we assume that there are five possible relevance labels, as is customary in web search settings [Sanderson, 2010], then this model has 11 parameters in total: five attractiveness, five satisfaction and one continuation parameter.

By training a model only once on a relatively small number of clicks, one can then reuse it with new datasets with completely different documents, provided that they have relevance judgements on the same scale.

If there is no click data available to estimate the values of the click model parameters, one can consider different assignments for these parameters. For instance, Hofmann et al. [2013] consider three different extreme cases for the attractiveness parameter assignment, which they call *perfect*, *navigational* and *informational* user models. Each of these user models corresponds

---

[3]http://webscope.sandbox.yahoo.com/catalog.php?datatype=c.
[4]http://imat2009.yandex.ru/academic/mathematic/2009/en/datasets.

to a different mapping from the relevance scale (Hofmann et al. use three relevance grades) to the probability of attractiveness. The intuition is that under the perfect user model only relevant documents are clicked, under the navigational user model there is some relaxation to this, while the informational user model assumes that a user carefully examines a SERP and can click even non-relevant documents with reasonable probability. The assignment of the attractiveness parameters according to [Hofmann et al., 2013] is given in the Table 8.1. By considering all three different models in a simulation, one may hope to cover real-world settings, which supposedly lie somewhere in between.

Table 8.1: Click model attractiveness parameters for the simulated click models from [Hofmann et al., 2013]

relevance grade	0	1	2
perfect model	0.00	0.50	1.00
navigational model	0.05	0.50	0.95
informational model	0.40	0.70	0.90

Using clicks and editorial relevance. Using both click signals and human relevance labels is a promising direction for click models, which can help to get more accurate predictions and to overcome data sparsity issues. The first steps in this direction are presented in the noise-aware framework due to Chen et al. [2012b]. In order to make use of editorial judgements, the notion of relevance R is introduced directly into the model. Then, the user's click given examination is either guided by relevance (noise-free environment, $N_r = 0$) or not (noisy environment, $N_r = 1$). Formally, this can be written as follows:

$$P(C_r = 1 \mid E_r = 0) = 0 \qquad (8.43)$$
$$P(C_r = 1 \mid E_r = 1, R_r = 1, N_r = 0) = \alpha_{u_r q} \qquad (8.44)$$
$$P(C_r = 1 \mid E_r = 1, R_r = 0, N_r = 0) = 0 \qquad (8.45)$$
$$P(C_r = 1 \mid E_r = 1, N_r = 1) = \beta_q, \qquad (8.46)$$

where β_q is a query-specific parameter.

The authors introduce two models, N-DBN and N-UBM, and show that they consistently have better perplexity than the corresponding baseline models. For details on the parameter estimation (that uses editorial relevance data) as well as on the estimation of the noise probability, we refer the reader to the original paper [Chen et al., 2012b].

8.6 NON-LINEAR SERP EXAMINATION

Aggregated search. It is evident that the more heterogeneous a SERP is, the more likely it is that a user is going to examine it in a non-linear way. We have already seen this when we discussed the VCM model by Wang et al. [2013a] in Section 8.1.2. In that model a user is allowed to jump right to a vertical block and then proceed up or down.

Temporal click models.   A similar idea is used for a range of temporal click models. Unlike most click models that are based on the position of search engine results, temporal click models are based on the time series of users' actions, such as clicks, examinations, etc., and therefore give us a different perspective on user interaction behavior.

In the setting of sponsored search, Xu et al. [2010] introduce the *temporal click model* (sometimes referred to as TCM, which should not be confused with the task-centric model, for which the same acronym is being used in the literature, see Section 8.2.2). The temporal click model builds on what the authors call the positional rationality hypothesis, according to which users first examine two ads together and assess their quality, and then compare their quality. The temporal click model is found to have better CTR prediction accuracy (Section 5.3) than BBM[5] on less frequent queries and comparable performance on frequent queries.

Wang et al. [2010] model the sequence of user actions on a SERP as a Markov chain and consider not only positional but also temporal information in search logs. The authors model all the user actions in a session, including hovering events, page loading and unloading, query reformulation, etc., in addition to conventional click events. The resulting model is compared against the experimental outcomes of an eye tracking study and high agreement is reported. No evaluation of the type that we focus on in this book (see Chapter 5) is performed. He and Wang [2011] refine this approach by explicitly modeling the duration of an event (e.g., the time a user spends reading a search result).

The *temporal hidden click model* (THCM) by Xu et al. [2012] also incorporates non-linear SERP examination, with a special focus on what the authors call revising patterns, where a user clicks on a higher-ranked document after having clicked on a lower-ranked one. Xu et al. suggest a temporal model in which, after examining a document u_r, a user examines the next document u_{r+1} with probability α, but may also examine the previous document u_{r-1} with probability γ. Several evaluations are conducted. In terms of perplexity (Section 5.2), THCM is found to outperform both DBM and CCM. In terms of relevance prediction (Section 5.4), there is no significant difference between THCM and DBM or CCM on frequent queries, but on moderately frequent and rare queries the authors do report significant improvements.

Recently, Wang et al. [2015] have introduced the *partially sequential click model* (PSCM). It builds on two hypotheses. The first, called the locally unidirectional examination assumption, says that between adjacent clicks, users tend to examine search results in a single direction without changes and this direction is usually consistent with that of clicks (whether going up or down the SERP). The second, called the non first-order examination assumption, says that although the examination behavior between adjacent clicks can be regarded as locally unidirectional, users may skip a few results and examine a result at some distance from the current one following a certain direction. PSCM outperforms existing models in terms of perplexity (Section 5.2) and relevance prediction (Section 5.4).

---

[5]We discuss the BBM model, which is due to Liu et al. [2009], in Section 4.4.

Switching between organic web and other SERP blocks. Finally, the *whole page click model* (WPC) by Chen et al. [2011] is meant to tackle the problem of side elements on a SERP, such as ads or related searches. The authors suggest to separately model two things: user transitions between blocks (organic results, top ads, side ads, related searches, etc.) and user behavior within a block. The first model, called macro-model, is set up as a Markov chain, while the second model, called micro-model, is based on a regular click model (Chen et al. use UBM). Since WPC considers additional SERP elements, it yields substantial perplexity improvements over the baseline model for the whole SERP as well as separately within the organic result block and ads block.

8.7 USING FEATURES

Regression-based models. Starting with the work of Richardson et al. [2007], a feature-based approach to predicting clicks in the setting of sponsored search has become popular. Richardson et al. suggest to use a feature-based logistic model that they train using conventional machine learning methods:

$$P(C_u = 1) = \frac{1}{1 + e^{-Z}} \qquad (8.47)$$

$$Z = \sum w_i f_i, \qquad (8.48)$$

where f_i is a feature extracted from the query, document and rank, and w_i is the weight of f_i learned during training. Richardson et al. use 81 features and show that their model predicts CTR better than the simple RCM model (Section 3.1).

Like logistic regression, factorization machines are a general regression model. They capture interactions between pairs of elements using factors. Factorization machines can efficiently model user interactions with various elements of ads. Rendel [2012] uses factorization machines and a broad range of user-, content- and interaction-based features to predict the CTR of an ad given a user and a query. This system produced very competitive results at the 2012 edition of the KDDCup.[6]

Recurrent neural networks have also been used for click prediction in sponsored search. Zhang et al. [2014] observe that users' interactions with ads depend on past user behavior in terms of what queries they submitted, what ads they clicked or ignored, how much time they spent on the landing pages of clicked ads, etc. Zhang et al. build on these observations and introduce a click prediction framework based on recurrent neural networks. This framework directly models the dependency on users' sequential behavior as a part of the click prediction process through the recurrent structure of a network. The authors compare their approach against logistic regression and non-recurrent neural networks and find that their method wins on the ad click prediction task in terms of the Area under the ROC Curve and Relative Information Gain scores.

---

[6]http://www.kddcup2012.org.

Post-click model (PCC).   Zhong et al. [2010] suggest to take into account the after-click behavior on a landing page and beyond. They start with the DBN model (Section 3.8) and add a feature-based term to the satisfaction probability (3.38) using the following formula:

$$P(S_r = 1 \mid C_r = 1) = P\left(\sigma_{u_r q} + \sum_i y_{u_r i} f_i + \epsilon > 0\right),$$ (8.49)

where $\sigma_{u_r q}$ is assumed to have a normal distribution, f_i is a post-click feature like "dwell time on the clicked page," "time before next query" or the fact of a search engine switch, $y_{u_r i}$ is a weight parameter and ϵ is a normally distributed error term.

The authors show that this model allows for efficient training and outperforms DBN and CCM in terms of the relevance prediction evaluation (Section 5.4).

General click model (GCM).   Zhu et al. [2010] propose to generalize the attributes on which model parameters depend. For example, in the DCM model (Section 3.6) the attractiveness parameter α_{uq} depends on a query-document pair while the continuation parameter λ_r depends on the current rank (also see Table 3.2). In the *general click model* (GCM), suggested by Zhu et al., click model parameters can depend on other attributes, such as time of the day, user browser, user location or length of a URL:

$$P(E_1 = 1) = 1$$ (8.50)
$$P(E_r = 1 \mid E_{r-1} = 0) = 0$$ (8.51)

$$P(C_r = 1 \mid E_r = 1) = P\left(\sum_t \theta_{f_t^{user}}^R + \sum_j \theta_{f_{i,j}^{url}}^R + \epsilon > 0\right)$$ (8.52)

$$P(E_r = 1 \mid E_{r-1} = 1, C_{r-1} = 0) = P\left(\sum_t \theta_{f_t^{user}}^A + \sum_j \theta_{f_{i,j}^{url}}^A + \epsilon > 0\right)$$ (8.53)

$$P(E_r = 1 \mid C_{r-1} = 1) = P\left(\sum_t \theta_{f_t^{user}}^B + \sum_j \theta_{f_{i,j}^{url}}^B + \epsilon > 0\right),$$ (8.54)

where f_t^{user} and $f_{i,j}^{url}$ are user-specific and URL-specific features respectively, θ_f is some random distribution parametrized by the corresponding feature and ϵ is a normally distributed error term (cf. (8.49)). By using appropriate features f and distributions θ_f it can be shown, that CM, DCM, CCM and DBN models can be considered as special cases of this model.

The authors show that a model with many attributes (they use between 7 and 21 attributes) the model performs better than DBN and CCM in terms of both log-likelihood (Section 5.1) and CTR prediction (Section 5.3).

Wang et al. [2013b] propose a similar model called Bayesian Sequential State model (BSS) that extends the feature set by adding features based on the dependencies between sequential click events. Their model has poor perplexity score, but outperforms UBM and DBN on the task of relevance prediction (Section 5.4). The authors did not, however, compare their model to GCM.

In this chapter we have covered a diverse landscape of recent click model developments. As the reader can see, most advanced models are built on top of the basic click models presented in Chapter 3. Quite often, performance improvements are achieved at the cost of far greater model complexity and, as usual, compromises have to be made between the improvement a newly proposed model brings and the amount of time required to implement and test this model and resources required to run it.

CHAPTER 9

Applications

In this chapter we expand on the main click model applications that were briefly mentioned in the introduction. We start with the most straightforward application, that of simulating users, which we discuss in Section 9.1. Then we move on to a more practical area of observing user behavior and drawing important conclusions about IR system design in Section 9.2. Next, we discuss a really powerful application of click models that allows one to improve search quality by correctly interpreting user clicks (Section 9.3). Finally, we show how click models can be applied to offline evaluation by incorporating user behavior into evaluation metrics (Section 9.4).

9.1 SIMULATING USERS

When we are performing online quality evaluation using methods such as A/B-testing [Kohavi et al., 2008] or interleaving [Chapelle et al., 2012], or assess the response time and resource requirements of a search system, we either need to have access to real users or somehow simulate them. It is clear that experimenting with real users is not always feasible or sufficient due to the limited amount of user interaction data, the sensitive nature of such data and the risk of noticeably degrading the user experience. Click models give a perfect solution to this problem: once trained on historical interaction data, a click model can be applied to simulate an infinite number of user clicks. This can be done using a very simple algorithm, as shown in Algorithm 1, where the probability $P(C_r = 1 \mid \mathbf{C}_{<r})$ of a click given the clicks above it is taken from Table 3.1 for each particular model.

As we will explain below, depending on the character and availability of training, there are different ways in which one can use click models for user simulations.

Simulating users in the same sessions: data expansion.   The first situation we consider is when we need to simulate clicks in the same sessions as we have in our training set. Assume, for example, that we are running a ranking experiment where, with a certain probability, a user is presented with a re-ordered set of results on a SERP. Due to the risk of degrading the user experience, re-orderings are shown with a very small probability. On the one hand, this prudent approach minimizes the impact on the search quality. On the other hand, it leads to fewer clicks on the experimental rankings, as a result of which we may have problems drawing conclusions using online click-based metrics. What we can do instead is to train a click model using available clicks in the sessions with re-orderings and extrapolate these clicks to the same SERPs to get more

---

Algorithm 1 Simulating user clicks for a query session.

Input: click model M, query session s
Output: vector of simulated clicks $(c_1, \ldots, c_n)$

1: **for** $r \leftarrow 1$ to $|s|$ **do**
2:    Compute $p \leftarrow P(C_r = 1 \mid C_1 = c_1, \ldots, C_{r-1} = c_{r-1})$ using previous clicks $c_1, \ldots, c_{r-1}$
     and the parameters of the model M
3:    Generate random value c_r from *Bernoulli(p)*
4: **end for**

---

robust estimations for quality metrics such as *abandonment rate* or *mean reciprocal rank* (MRR) [Radlinski et al., 2008].

Simulating users in new sessions.   Quite often, one needs to extrapolate user behavior to unseen data. For example, one may want to test a completely new ranking of documents and does not want to show this ranking to real users. Here, click models can be of great help because they essentially decompose the click probability into the properties of a document (such as attractiveness or satisfaction parameters) and the effects of the document rank and surrounding documents. Consequently, even if a click model was trained on one ranking of documents, we can simulate user clicks on different rankings of the same documents. We can go even further and apply a trained click model to unseen documents or queries. In this case, models such as the matrix factorization model (MFCM) by Shen et al. [2012] can help to fill the gaps in the sparse matrix of model parameters.

Simulating users on the LETOR datasets.   Often, a click model has to be applied to a totally new dataset that does not share common queries or documents with previously used ones or it is hard to match those because they are anonymized in different ways. This often happens in the setting of academic research labs that do not have access to large-scale search logs, but also with commercial organizations that want to quickly assess their ideas on new data using click logs. Here, editorial relevance labels can serve as a link between different datasets. As we discussed in Section 8.5, every click model can be modified in such a way that its parameters depend only on the rank and editorial relevance label of documents. In this manner we not only contract the size of a trained model to the order of hundreds of parameters, but also allow researchers to exchange these parameters without sharing the data the model was trained on.

Once relevance-based click model parameters have been made available, they can then be applied to other datasets that have relevance labels. Typically, these are datasets used for learning to rank (LETOR)—a task for machine learning to rank documents in a way that optimizes some utility function. A number of such datasets have been published, for example, by Microsoft

Research Asia[1] [Liu et al., 2007, Qin et al., 2010]. The algorithm for simulating clicks in this setting is the following: train a click model on a dataset having both clicks and relevance labels (see Table 6.1) and then apply it to any dataset having only relevance labels.

Such relevance-based click models have been used successfully to simulate users in interleaving experiments [Chuklin et al., 2013a, 2015, Hofmann et al., 2011, 2013].

9.2   USER INTERACTION ANALYSIS

One of the less obvious applications of click models is their usage as an observational device in the area of user experience research (UX). By examining parameters of a click model one can learn more about user behavior and make changes to user interfaces based on insights gained in this manner.

Dupret and Piwowarski [2008] are the first to point out this application of click models. In particular, they analyze the value of the examination parameter $\gamma_{rr'}$ of the UBM model (Section 3.5). This parameter defines the probability of examining a document at rank r, given that the previous click was at rank r'. The authors present a set of results that confirm the fact that the examination probability declines with the rank r of the current document, but also show that this probability exhibits a non-trivial dependency on the rank of the previous click r'.

Analyzing this kind of information is especially interesting in the case of aggregated search, which we studied in Section 8.1. By looking at the parameters of a click model we can quantify how vertical documents affect the way a user consumes a SERP. Following that, one may introduce changes to the way we surface these vertical results. For example, Chen et al. [2012a] show that the presence of vertical documents affects the examination of the neighboring web documents; the effect is less prominent for textual verticals like News, which only affects its neighbors when it is placed at the top. But if, for example, an Image vertical is placed at rank 4, then web documents at ranks 5, 6 and 7 will have substantially higher chances of being examined than without the placement of the Image vertical.

9.3   INFERENCE OF DOCUMENT RELEVANCE

One of the ways to define document relevance is through the probability of user satisfaction given examination $P(S_r = 1 \mid E_r = 1)$, as was suggested by Chapelle and Zhang [2009]. Having trained a click model which has the notion of satisfaction, one can obtain this probability from the click model parameters:

$$R_{u_r q} = P(S_r = 1 \mid E_r = 1) = P(S_r = 1 \mid C_r = 1) \cdot P(C_r = 1 \mid E_r = 1). \tag{9.1}$$

After having obtained this click-based relevance score, we can either use it to evaluate the quality of the current production system using metrics such as DCG [Järvelin and Kekäläinen, 2002] or use it to improve the system in the future. Chapelle and Zhang [2009] show that if this click-based

---

[1]http://research.microsoft.com/en-us/um/beijing/projects/letor/.

relevance is used as a learning feature in a machine learning-based ranking system, it significantly improves the end result, which means that it is a powerful signal of document quality.

Ozertem et al. [2011] use this notion of click-based relevance together with a smoothing technique to complement editorial relevance judgments in the evaluation process. They show that despite a fair amount of missing judgements, a significant correlation with the ground-truth DCG can be achieved.

9.4　CLICK MODEL-BASED METRICS

Here we discuss the connection between click models and web search quality metrics. In the so-called Cranfield approach described and practiced by Cleverdon et al. [1966], the relevance of each query-document pair is obtained from trained raters independently of other documents. This way the same relevance labels can be used to evaluate different rankings of documents, which makes it an effective way to evaluate systems without running long and costly experiments or user studies. On the other hand, these relevance labels need to be aggregated in a SERP-level quality metric, which is not a straightforward task.

The first metric to evaluate the quality of a whole SERP was just a simple precision metric: the number of relevant documents found by raters divided by the total number of documents shown to a user. With the emergence of ubiquitous search engines that are being used many times a day it has become clear that users do not always examine all documents, but rather start from top to bottom. Following this idea, Järvelin and Kekäläinen [2002] suggest a discounted metric, DCG that assigns higher weights to the documents higher in the ranking. However, this metric does not fully explain why this particular rank discount has to be used nor does it address the question of dealing with graded relevance. For instance, is it better to have two marginally relevant documents at ranks 2 and 3 or one very relevant document at rank 3? In order to answer this question, one must first observe user behavior and learn regularities from it.

Following early attempts to build user behavior-aware evaluation metrics such as Expected Reciprocal Rank (ERR) by Chapelle et al. [2009] and Expected Browser Utility (EBU) by Yilmaz et al. [2010], Chuklin et al. [2013c] suggest the idea that any click model can be a basis for building evaluation metrics. Following Carterette [2011], Chuklin et al. suggest to use two families of click model-based metrics: utility-based and effort-based. Utility-based metrics assume that by examining relevant documents a user accumulates utility, so the metric should be defined as an average utility value:

$$uMetric = \sum_{r=1}^{n} P(C_r = 1) \cdot U_r, \tag{9.2}$$

where U_r is some utility measure of the r-th document (usually relevance R_r). So if we fix a click model and compute click probabilities $P(C_r = 1)$ for a particular SERP we can plug them into the above formula and obtain an evaluation metric.

There are two important factors to note here. First, a click model used has to be relevance-based (see Section 8.5) in order for the final metric to depend only on the relevance of documents on a SERP. Second, the click probability has to be the full click probability, i.e., it has to be derived from the model equations such that it is marginalized over all random variables that are not observed (note that clicks are also not observed when we want to apply a metric). For instance, for UBM (Section 3.5) this requires marginalizing over all possible ranks of the previous click. We give more details and provide final formulas in Section 3.9.

As to the family of so-called effort-based metrics, they are based on models, such as DBN (Section 3.8) and DCM (Section 3.6), that have the notion of satisfaction. The metric then computes the average effort a searcher has to spend until they get satisfied:

$$eMetric = \sum_{r=1}^{n} P(S_r = 1) \cdot F_r, \tag{9.3}$$

where F_r is some effort measure. Usually, the inverse of an effort, such as, e.g., reciprocal rank $\frac{1}{r}$ is used, so that the higher metric values correspond to lower effort. For example, the widely used ERR metric by Chapelle et al. [2009] can be viewed as a metric of this family.

Chuklin et al. [2013c] find that an effort-based metric based on UBM shows the highest correlation with online experiments, especially in the case where there is a lot of unlabeled data. However, in some cases other models may be more suitable. For example, when we consider aggregated search, there exist more precise click models that we have discussed in Section 8.1. As has been shown by Markov et al. [2014], in the presence of vertical results, metrics based on click models for aggregated search show better alignment with online user preferences.

Similarly, Kharitonov et al. [2013] consider a problem of evaluating query auto-completion where a specific user model needs to be used. They also demonstrate that incorporating a user model into evaluation helps to achieve higher correlation with online metrics.

CHAPTER 10

Discussion and Directions for Future Work

In this book we have presented a coherent view on the area of click models for web search. The main focus of the book is on models represented as probabilistic graphical models (PGMs). Using the terminology of Koller and Friedman [2009], most of the models studied in the book are directed *Bayesian networks* (see Definition 2.1). As we have shown, this machinery is very powerful and allows one to express many ideas about user behavior, incorporate additional signals and achieve good performance results. But of course, there is always room for improvement. Specifically, we believe that the development of user modeling should go in three directions.

Foundations of user modeling. The first direction is to expand the foundations of the user modeling aspects of click models. As we have seen in Chapter 7, greater complexity does not always come with better results. Nevertheless, there are many approaches to user modeling that have not been tried yet. First of all, the area of probabilistic graphical models itself suggests additional tools such as undirected Markov networks or partially directed conditional random fields [Koller and Friedman, 2009, Chapter 4]. These alternative structures allow us to specify fewer dependencies between user's behavioral states. Also, there are many options to generalize conditional probability distributions. Currently, we set the probability of observing some state to have a simple dependency on the states connected to it in a PGM. We may extend this by using so-called structured probability distributions where the dependency becomes more complex; see [Koller and Friedman, 2009, Chapter 5]. This extension would allow us to naturally introduce feature-based machine learning elements as in some of the models that we discussed in Section 8.7.

Another promising approach is structure learning [Koller and Friedman, 2009, Chapter 18]. Up until now we always fixed the structure of a network. However, the very fact that we have so many different models, as demonstrated in this book, suggests that we, humans, cannot easily engineer a perfect dependency graph by hand. Instead, we may want to infer this structure from data, just as we currently do for model parameters. The recent successes of distributed representations in many prediction tasks suggest a natural way forward, viz. to represent user behavior as a sequence of vector states that capture user interactions with a SERP; see, e.g., [Zhang et al., 2014].

Rich interactions and alternative search environments. As we pointed out in Section 8.4, even in a desktop environment, there are additional signals that one may use to gain a better understanding of user interactions with a SERP. While cognitively rich signals such as eye tracking and mouse movements increasingly receive attention, other, perhaps more mundane, aspects have been little studied, as a typical SERP may not be equipped with such aspects. Pagination buttons, as discussed in Section 8.2.1, are but one example. Other examples include interface elements to support result list refinement through facets and filters [He et al., 2015], common in professional search environments [Huurnink et al., 2010], so-called knowledge cards [Blanco et al., 2013] and interactive elements such as weather or calculator widgets.

Devices beyond desktop computers provide other means of interaction with search results. Mobile devices mainly rely on touch technology, which substitutes mouse movements and page scrolls and supports a number of gestures. Voice input is also more heavily used for mobile search interfaces. Also, it was shown recently that a SERP viewport (the visible portion of a web page) is an important signal of a searcher's attention on mobile devices [Lagun et al., 2014]. Other devices, such as TV sets, provide limited interaction capabilities, but may have additional search elements, such as preview, which are not available in standard search environments. As Markov et al. [2015] put it, the main challenge here is to capture and reliably interpret user signals other than clicks. For example, when capturing mouse movements and touch gestures, one needs to map the position of a cursor/finger on a screen to an underlying object on a SERP. Also, while some user signals have relatively clear interpretations (e.g., clicks, scrolls, zooming), others do not (e.g., mouse movements).

Apart from the fact that different devices provide different means of interaction with search results, devices may also differ in their technical characteristics and main function. Desktops and laptops are general-purpose devices with rich interaction capabilities, and hence they can be used for most types of search. In contrast, smartphones and tablet computers are more mobile and have additional components, such as a touch screen, microphone and GPS, which make them perfect for specific types of search, e.g., local search. Search systems on devices such as TV sets and GPS navigation devices, may use additional input sources, such as voice commands, user location or automobile sensors. On the other hand, they provide limited search capabilities and are often geared toward answering specific types of question. Thus, the device type determines not only the way of interaction with search results, but also the user's search intents. The notion of what constitutes a successful search may also be different on different devices. In generic web search, a successful session is usually one with many clicks followed by long dwell time. In TV search, however, a successful session could be one that ends with a purchase of a TV program. Similarly, a successful search session on a GPS-navigation device should probably be followed by the user navigating to a point of interest [Norouzzadeh Ravari et al., 2015]. Overall, users' search behavior is bound to differ considerably between devices. Therefore, models aimed at capturing and predicting user behavior have to carefully consider special properties of each device and corresponding user intents and indicators of success.

Convergence.   A final direction for future development consists of fusions of ideas developed in adjacent areas. We already discussed some of these ideas in Chapter 8, but there is more to it. First, there is a large body of work on user modeling and user behavior analysis for online advertising and sponsored search; see, e.g., [Alipov et al., 2014, Ashkan and Clarke, 2012, Ghosh and Mahdian, 2008, Graepel et al., 2010, Richardson et al., 2007, Xiong et al., 2012, Zhu et al., 2010]. Since predicting clicks is critical for many commercial search and advertisement applications, models aimed at predicting clicks appeared relatively early on in those areas [Richardson et al., 2007]. Since then, they developed rather independently from click models for web search. Yin et al. [2014] add organic results to a click model for ads, but only as an external entity. We believe that these two areas could and should benefit more from each other and that they will eventually converge.

There are also some more distant areas, such as user experience studies [Dumais et al., 2001], network and game theory [Easley and Kleinberg, 2010] and learning to rank [Burges et al., 2005] that contribute ideas to the area of user modeling and will continue to do so in the future.

As we have shown in Section 8.3, there is a fair amount of work that tries to tackle the problem of user diversity. The next steps in the direction of personalization should concern the aggregation of similar users into clusters [Buscher et al., 2012] or cohorts [Hassan and White, 2013] in order to improve model performance for infrequent users and to minimize overfitting risks.

Bibliography

Vyacheslav Alipov, Valery Topinsky, and Ilya Trofimov. On peculiarities of positional effects in sponsored search. In *SIGIR*, 2014. ACM Press. DOI: 10.1145/2600428.2609498. 83

Jaime Arguello, Fernando Diaz, Jamie Callan, and Jean-François Crespo. Sources of evidence for vertical selection. In *SIGIR*. ACM Press, 2009. DOI: 10.1145/1571941.1571997. 48

Jaime Arguello, Fernando Diaz, and Milad Shokouhi. Integrating and ranking aggregated content on the web. In *WWW*. ACM Press, 2012. Tutorial at WWW 2012. 48

Azin Ashkan and Charles L.A. Clarke. Modeling browsing behavior for click analysis in sponsored search. In *CIKM*, 2012. ACM Press. DOI: 10.1145/2396761.2398563. 45, 66, 83

Christopher M. Bishop. *Pattern Recognition and Machine Learning*. Springer, 2006. 3

Roi Blanco, Berkant Barla Cambazoglu, Peter Mika, and Nicolas Torzec. Entity recommendations in web search. In *The Semantic Web–ISWC 2013*. Springer, 2013. DOI: 10.1007/978-3-642-41338-4_3. 82

Chris Burges, Tal Shaked, Erin Renshaw, Ari Lazier, Matt Deeds, Nicole Hamilton, and Greg Hullender. Learning to rank using gradient descent. In *ICML*, 2005. ACM Press. DOI: 10.1145/1102351.1102363. 83

Georg Buscher, Ryen W. White, Susan Dumais, and Jeff Huang. Large-scale analysis of individual and task differences in search result page examination strategies. In *WSDM*, 2012. ACM Press. DOI: 10.1145/2124295.2124341. 83

Ben Carterette. System effectiveness, user models, and user utility: A conceptual framework for investigation. In *SIGIR*. ACM, 2011. DOI: 10.1145/2009916.2010037. 78

Olivier Chapelle and Ya Zhang. A dynamic bayesian network click model for web search ranking. In *WWW*, 2009. ACM Press. DOI: 10.1145/1526709.1526711. 2, 16, 17, 23, 30, 33, 45, 46, 47, 51, 77

Olivier Chapelle, Donald Metzler, Ya Zhang, and Pierre Grinspan. Expected reciprocal rank for graded relevance. In *CIKM*, 2009. ACM Press. DOI: 10.1145/1645953.1646033. 78, 79

Olivier Chapelle, Thorsten Joachims, Filip Radlinski, and Yisong Yue. Large-scale validation and analysis of interleaved search evaluation. *ACM Transactions on Information Systems*, 2012. DOI: 10.1145/2094072.2094078. 75

Danqi Chen, Weizhu Chen, Haixun Wang, Zheng Chen, and Qiang Yang. Beyond ten blue links: enabling user click modeling in federated web search. In *WSDM*, 2012a. ACM Press. DOI: 10.1145/2124295.2124351. 1, 2, 48, 51, 61, 62, 63, 77

Mon Chu Chen, John R. Anderson, and Myeong Ho Sohn. What can a mouse cursor tell us more?: Correlation of eye/mouse movements on web browsing. In *CHI'01 extended abstracts on Human factors in computing systems*, 2001. ACM Press. DOI: 10.1145/634067.634234. 68

Weizhu Chen, Zhanglong Ji, Si Shen, and Qiang Yang. A whole page click model to better interpret search engine click data. In *AAAI*. AAAI Press, 2011. 72

Weizhu Chen, Dong Wang, Yuchen Zhang, Zheng Chen, Adish Singla, and Qiang Yang. A noise-aware click model for web search. In *WSDM*, 2012b. ACM Press. DOI: 10.1145/2124295.2124335. 6, 70

Aleksandr Chuklin, Anne Schuth, Katja Hofmann, Pavel Serdyukov, and Maarten de Rijke. Evaluating aggregated search using interleaving. In *CIKM*, 2013a. ACM Press. DOI: 10.1145/2505515.2505698. 77

Aleksandr Chuklin, Pavel Serdyukov, and Maarten de Rijke. Using intent information to model user behavior in diversified search. In *ECIR*, 2013b. DOI: 10.1007/978-3-642-36973-5_1. 2, 48, 51, 63, 66

Aleksandr Chuklin, Pavel Serdyukov, and Maarten de Rijke. Click model-based information retrieval metrics. In *SIGIR*, 2013c. ACM Press. DOI: 10.1145/2484028.2484071. 19, 78, 79

Aleksandr Chuklin, Pavel Serdyukov, and Maarten de Rijke. Modeling clicks beyond the first result page. In *CIKM*, 2013d. ACM Press. DOI: 10.1145/2505515.2507859. 44, 45, 64

Aleksandr Chuklin, Ke Zhou, Anne Schuth, Floor Sietsma, and Maarten de Rijke. Evaluating intuitiveness of vertical-aware click models. In *SIGIR*, 2014. ACM Press. DOI: 10.1145/2600428.2609513. 47, 48, 62

Aleksandr Chuklin, Anne Schuth, Ke Zhou, and Maarten de Rijke. A comparative analysis of interleaving methods for aggregated search. *ACM Transactions on Information Systems*, 33(2), 2015. DOI: 10.1145/2668120. 62, 77

Cyril W. Cleverdon, Jack Mills, and Michael Keen. Aslib Cranfield research project - Factors determining the performance of indexing systems; Volume 1, Design; Part 1, text. Technical report, College of Aeronautics, Cranfield, 1966. 78

Nick Craswell, Onno Zoeter, Michael Taylor, and Bill Ramsey. An experimental comparison of click position-bias models. In *WSDM*, 2008. ACM Press. DOI: 10.1145/1341531.1341545. 2, 9, 10, 11, 12, 43

Arthur P. Dempster, Nan M. Laird, and Donald B. Rubin. Maximum likelihood from incomplete data via the EM algorithm. *Journal of the royal statistical society. Series B (methodological)*, 1977. 27, 28

Fernando Diaz, Ryen W. White, Georg Buscher, and Dan Liebling. Robust models of mouse movement on dynamic web search results pages. In *CIKM*, 2013. ACM Press. DOI: 10.1145/2505515.2505717. 2, 68

Zhicheng Dou, Ruihua Song, and Ji-Rong Wen. A large-scale evaluation and analysis of personalized search strategies. In *WWW*, 2007. ACM Press. DOI: 10.1145/1242572.1242651. 2

Susan Dumais, Edward Cutrell, and Hao Chen. Optimizing search by showing results in context. In *CHI*, 2001. ACM Press. DOI: 10.1145/365024.365116. 83

Georges Dupret and Ciya Liao. A model to estimate intrinsic document relevance from the clickthrough logs of a web search engine. In *WSDM*, 2010. ACM Press. DOI: 10.1145/1718487.1718510. 47

Georges Dupret, Vanessa Murdock, and Benjamin Piwowarski. Web search engine evaluation using clickthrough data and a user model. In *WWW*, 2007. ACM Press. 2

Georges E. Dupret and Benjamin Piwowarski. A user browsing model to predict search engine click data from past observations. In *SIGIR*, 2008. ACM Press. DOI: 10.1145/1390334.1390392. 2, 9, 10, 13, 30, 43, 44, 45, 51, 77

David Easley and Jon Kleinberg. *Networks, Crowds, and Markets: Reasoning About a Highly Connected World*. Cambridge University Press, 2010. 83

Bradley Efron and R J Tibshirani. *An Introduction to the Bootstrap (Chapman & Hall/CRC Monographs on Statistics & Applied Probability)*. Chapman and Hall/CRC, 1 edition, May 1994. 53

Ronald Aylmer Fisher. On the mathematical foundations of theoretical statistics. *Philosophical Transactions of the Royal Society of London. Series A, Containing Papers of a Mathematical or Physical Character*, 1922. DOI: 10.1098/rsta.1922.0009. 43

Arpita Ghosh and Mohammad Mahdian. Externalities in online advertising. In *WWW*, 2008. ACM Press. DOI: 10.1145/1367497.1367520. 83

Thore Graepel, Joaquin Q. Candela, Thomas Borchert, and Ralf Herbrich. Web-scale bayesian click-through rate prediction for sponsored search advertising in microsoft's bing search engine. In *ICML*. ACM Press, 2010. 83

Artem Grotov, Aleksandr Chuklin, Ilya Markov, Luka Stout, Finde Xumara, and Maarten de Rijke. A Comparative Study of Click Models for Web Search. In *CLEF*, 2015. 59

Zhiwei Guan and Edward Cutrell. An eye tracking study of the effect of target rank on web search. In *CHI*, 2007. ACM Press. DOI: 10.1145/1240624.1240691. 1

Fan Guo, Chao Liu, Anitha Kannan, Tom Minka, Michael Taylor, Yi-Min Wang, and Christos Faloutsos. Click chain model in web search. In *WWW*, 2009a. ACM Press. DOI: 10.1145/1526709.1526712. 14, 30, 44, 45, 66

Fan Guo, Chao Liu, and Yi Min Wang. Efficient multiple-click models in web search. In *WSDM*, 2009b. ACM Press. DOI: 10.1145/1498759.1498818. 2, 14, 25, 26, 45, 51, 53

Ahmed Hassan and Ryen W. White. Personalized models of search satisfaction. In *CIKM*, 2013. ACM Press. DOI: 10.1145/2505515.2505681. 83

Jiyin He, Marc Bron, Arjen P. de Vries, Leif Azzopardi, and Maarten de Rijke. Untangling result list refinement and ranking quality: A model for evaluation and prediction. In *SIGIR*, August 2015. ACM Press. 82

Yin He and Kuansan Wang. Inferring search behaviors using partially observable markov model with duration (pomd). In *WSDM*, 2011. ACM Press. DOI: 10.1145/1935826.1935891. 71

Katja Hofmann, Shimon Whiteson, and Maarten de Rijke. A probabilistic method for inferring preferences from clicks. In *CIKM*, 2011. ACM Press. DOI: 10.1145/2063576.2063618. 69, 77

Katja Hofmann, Anne Schuth, Shimon Whiteson, and Maarten de Rijke. Reusing historical interaction data for faster online learning to rank for IR. In *WSDM*, 2013. ACM Press. DOI: 10.1145/2433396.2433419. 69, 70, 77

Botao Hu, Yuchen Zhang, Weizhu Chen, Gang Wang, and Qiang Yang. Characterizing search intent diversity into click models. In *WWW*, 2011. ACM Press. DOI: 10.1145/1963405.1963412. 65

Jeff Huang, Ryen W. White, and Susan Dumais. No clicks, no problem: Using cursor movements to understand and improve search. In *CHI*, 2011. ACM Press. DOI: 10.1145/1978942.1979125. 68

Jeff Huang, Ryen W. White, Georg Buscher, and Kuansan Wang. Improving searcher models using mouse cursor activity. In *SIGIR*, 2012. ACM Press. DOI: 10.1145/2348283.2348313. 2, 68

Bouke Huurnink, Laura Hollink, Wietske van den Heuvel, and Maarten de Rijke. Search behavior of media professionals at an audiovisual archive: A transaction log analysis. *Journal of
the American Society for Information Science and Technology*, 61(6):1180–1197, June 2010. DOI:
10.1002/asi.21327. 82

Kalervo Järvelin and Jaana Kekäläinen. Cumulated gain-based evaluation of IR techniques. *ACM
Transactions on Information Systems*, 20(4):422–446, 2002. DOI: 10.1145/582415.582418. 47,
77, 78

Thorsten Joachims, Laura Granka, Bing Pan, Helene Hembrooke, and Geri Gay. Accurately
interpreting clickthrough data as implicit feedback. In *SIGIR*, 2005. ACM Press. DOI:
10.1145/1076034.1076063. 1, 2, 10, 11

Eugene Kharitonov, Craig Macdonald, Pavel Serdyukov, and Iadh Ounis. User model-
based metrics for offline query suggestion evaluation. In *SIGIR*, 2013. ACM Press. DOI:
10.1145/2484028.2484041. 79

Ron Kohavi, Roger Longbotham, Dan Sommerfield, and Randal M. Henne. Controlled experiments on the web: survey and practical guide. *Data Mining and Knowledge Discovery*, 18(1):
140–181, July 2008. DOI: 10.1007/s10618-008-0114-1. 45, 75

Ron Kohavi, Alex Deng, and Roger Longbotham. Seven rules of thumb for web site experi-
menters. In *KDD*, 2014. ACM Press. DOI: 10.1145/2623330.2623341. 1

Daphne Koller and Nir Friedman. *Probabilistic Graphical Models: Principles and Techniques*. MIT
Press, August 2009. 3, 6, 27, 81

Solomon Kullback and Richard A. Leibler. On information and sufficiency. *The Annals of Mathematical Statistics*, 22(1):79–86, 03 1951. DOI: 10.1214/aoms/1177729694. 46

Dmitry Lagun, Chih-Hung Hsieh, Dale Webster, and Vidhya Navalpakkam. Towards better
measurement of attention and satisfaction in mobile search. In *SIGIR*, 2014. ACM Press.
DOI: 10.1145/2600428.2609631. 82

Chao Liu, Fan Guo, and Christos Faloutsos. BBM: Bayesian browsing model from petabyte-
scale data. In *KDD*, 2009. ACM Press. DOI: 10.1145/1557019.1557081. 42, 51, 71

Tie-Yan Liu. Learning to rank for information retrieval. *Foundations and Trends in Information
Retrieval*, 3(3):225–331, 2009. DOI: 10.1561/1500000016. 47

Tie-Yan Liu, Jun Xu, Tao Qin, Wenying Xiong, and Hang Li. LETOR: Benchmark dataset for
research on learning to rank for information retrieval. In *SIGIR 2007 workshop on learning to
rank for information retrieval*, 2007. ACM Press. DOI: 10.1007/s10791-009-9123-y. 69, 77

Yiqun Liu, Chao Wang, Ke Zhou, Jianyun Nie, Min Zhang, and Shaoping Ma. From skimming to reading: A two-stage examination model for web search. In *CIKM*, 2014. ACM Press. DOI: 10.1145/2661829.2661907. 68

Lori Lorigo, Maya Haridasan, Hrönn Brynjarsdóttir, Ling Xia, Thorsten Joachims, Geri Gay, Laura Granka, Fabio Pellacini, and Bing Pan. Eye tracking and online search: Lessons learned and challenges ahead. *Journal of the American Society for Information Science and Technology*, 59 (7):1041–1052, 2008. DOI: 10.1002/asi.20794. 1

Ilya Markov, Eugene Kharitonov, Vadim Nikulin, Pavel Serdyukov, Maarten de Rijke, and Fabio Crestani. Vertical-aware click model-based effectiveness metrics. In *CIKM*, 2014. ACM Press. DOI: 10.1145/2661829.2661944. 79

Ilya Markov, Aleksandr Chuklin, and Yiqun Liu. Modeling search behavior in heterogeneous environments. In *Proceedings of HIA*, February 2015. ACM Press. 82

Alistair Moffat and Justin Zobel. Rank-biased precision for measurement of retrieval effectiveness. *ACM Transactions on Information Systems*, 27(1):1–27, December 2008. DOI: 10.1145/1416950.1416952. 2

Kevin Patrick Murphy. *Machine Learning: A Probabilistic Perspective*. MIT Press, 2013. 3, 43

Yaser Norouzzadeh Ravari, Ilya Markov, Artem Grotov, Maarten Clements, and Maarten de Rijke. User behavior in location search on mobile devices. In *ECIR*. Springer, April 2015. DOI: 10.1007/978-3-319-16354-3_79. 82

Umut Ozertem, Rosie Jones, and Benoit Dumoulin. Evaluating new search engine configurations with pre-existing judgments and clicks. In *WWW*, 2011. ACM. DOI: 10.1145/1963405.1963463. 78

Tao Qin, Tie-Yan Liu, Jun Xu, and Hang Li. Letor: A benchmark collection for research on learning to rank for information retrieval. *Information Retrieval*, 13(4):346–374, 2010. DOI: 10.1007/s10791-009-9123-y. 77

Filip Radlinski and Nick Craswell. Optimized interleaving for online retrieval evaluation. In *WSDM*, 2013. ACM Press. DOI: 10.1145/2433396.2433429. 46

Filip Radlinski, Madhu Kurup, and Thorsten Joachims. How does clickthrough data reflect retrieval quality? In *CIKM*, 2008. ACM Press. DOI: 10.1145/1458082.1458092. 76

Steffen Rendel. Social network and click-through prediction with factorization machines. In *KDD Cup Workshop*, 2012. ACM Press. 72

Matthew Richardson, Ewa Dominowska, and Robert Ragno. Predicting clicks: Estimating the click-through rate for new ads. In *WWW*, 2007. ACM Press. DOI: 10.1145/1242572.1242643. 45, 72, 83

Kerry Rodden, Xin Fu, Anne Aula, and Ian Spiro. Eye-mouse coordination patterns on web search results pages. In *CHI*, 2008. DOI: 10.1145/1358628.1358797. 68

Mark Sanderson. Test collection based evaluation of information retrieval systems. *Foundations and Trends in Information Retrieval*, 4(4):247–375, 2010. DOI: 10.1561/1500000009. 69

Anne Schuth, Katja Hofmann, Shimon Whiteson, and Maarten de Rijke. Lerot: An online learning to rank framework. In *Living Labs'13: Workshop on Living Labs for Information Retrieval Evaluation*, November 2013. ACM Press. DOI: 10.1145/2513150.2513162. 52

Pavel Serdyukov, Georges Dupret, and Nick Craswell. WSCD2013: Workshop on web search click data 2013. In *WSDM*, 2013. ACM Press. DOI: 10.1145/2433396.2433503. 50

Pavel Serdyukov, Georges Dupret, and Nick Craswell. Log-based personalization: The 4th web search click data (WSCD) workshop. In *WSDM*, 2014. ACM. DOI: 10.1145/2556195.2556207. 50

Si Shen, Botao Hu, Weizhu Chen, and Qiang Yang. Personalized click model through collaborative filtering. In *WSDM*, 2012. ACM Press. DOI: 10.1145/2124295.2124336. 42, 66, 76

Jaime Teevan, Susan T. Dumais, and Eric Horvitz. Personalizing search via automated analysis of interests and activities. In *SIGIR*, 2005. ACM Press. DOI: 10.1145/1076034.1076111. 2

Andrew Turpin, Falk Scholer, Kalervo Järvelin, Mingfang Wu, and J. Shane Culpepper. Including summaries in system evaluation. In *SIGIR*, 2009. ACM Press. DOI: 10.1145/1571941.1572029. 11, 69

Ellen M. Voorhees and Donna Harman. Overview of TREC 2001. In *TREC*. NIST, 2001. 69

Chao Wang, Yiqun Liu, Min Zhang, Shaoping Ma, Meihong Zheng, Jing Qian, and Kuo Zhang. Incorporating vertical results into search click models. In *SIGIR*, 2013a. ACM Press. DOI: 10.1145/2484028.2484036. 1, 2, 48, 62, 63, 70

Chao Wang, Yiqun Liu, Meng Wang, Ke Zhou, Jian-Yun Nie, and Shaoping Ma. Incorporating non-sequential behavior into click models. In *SIGIR*, 2015. ACM. DOI: 10.1145/2124295.2124334. 47, 71

Hongning Wang, ChengXiang Zhai, Anlei Dong, and Yi Chang. Content-aware click modeling. In *WWW*, 2013b. 73

Kuansan Wang, Nikolas Gloy, and Xiaolong Li. Inferring search behaviors using partially observable markov (pom) model. In *WSDM*, 2010. ACM Press. DOI: 10.1145/1718487.1718514. 71

Ryen W. White and Steven M. Drucker. Investigating behavioral variability in web search. In *WWW*, 2007. ACM Press. DOI: 10.1145/1242572.1242576. 65

Ian H. Witten and Eibe Frank. *Data Mining: Practical machine learning tools and techniques.* Morgan Kaufmann, 2005. 6

Qianli Xing, Yiqun Liu, Jian-Yun Nie, Min Zhang, Shaoping Ma, and Kuo Zhang. Incorporating user preferences into click models. In *CIKM*, 2013. ACM Press. DOI: 10.1145/2505515.2505704. 2, 46, 47, 67

Chenyan Xiong, Taifeng Wang, Wenkui Ding, Yidong Shen, and Tie-Yan Liu. Relational click prediction for sponsored search. In *WSDM*, 2012. ACM Press. DOI: 10.1145/2124295.2124355. 83

Danqing Xu, Yiqun Liu, Min Zhang, Shaoping Ma, and Liyun Ru. Incorporating revisiting behaviors into click models. In *WSDM*, 2012. ACM Press. DOI: 10.1145/2124295.2124334. 71

Wanhong Xu, Eren Manavoglu, and Erick Cantu-Paz. Temporal click model for sponsored search. In *SIGIR*, 2010. ACM Press. DOI: 10.1145/1835449.1835470. 71

Emine Yilmaz, Milad Shokouhi, Nick Craswell, and Stephen Robertson. Expected browsing utility for web search evaluation. In *CIKM*, 2010. ACM Press. DOI: 10.1145/1871437.1871672. 78

Dawei Yin, Shike Mei, Bin Cao, Jian-Tao Sun, and Brian D. Davison. Exploiting contextual factors for click modeling in sponsored search. In *WSDM*, 2014. ACM Press. DOI: 10.1145/2556195.2556237. 51, 83

Yuchen Zhang, Dong Wang, Gang Wang, Weizhu Chen, Zhihua Zhang, Botao Hu, and Li Zhang. Learning click models via probit bayesian inference. In *CIKM*, 2010. ACM Press. DOI: 10.1145/1871437.1871496. 42, 51

Yuchen Zhang, Weizhu Chen, Dong Wang, and Qiang Yang. User-click modeling for understanding and predicting search-behavior. In *KDD*, 2011. ACM Press. DOI: 10.1145/2020408.2020613. 1, 5, 64, 65

Yuyu Zhang, Hanjun Dai, Chang Xu, Jun Feng, Taifeng Wang, Jiang Bian, Bin Wang, and Tie-Yan Liu. Sequential click prediction for sponsored search with recurrent neural networks. In *AAAI*. AAAI Press, 2014. 72, 81

Feimin Zhong, Dong Wang, Gang Wang, Weizhu Chen, Yuchen Zhang, Zheng Chen, and Haixun Wang. Incorporating post-click behaviors into a click model. In *SIGIR*, 2010. ACM Press. DOI: 10.1145/1835449.1835510. 73

Ke Zhou, Mounia Lalmas, Tetsuya Sakai, Ronan Cummins, and Joemon M. Jose. On the reliability and intuitiveness of aggregated search metrics. In *CIKM*, 2013. ACM Press. DOI: 10.1145/2505515.2505691. 48

Zeyuan Allen Zhu, Weizhu Chen, Tom Minka, Chenguang Zhu, and Zheng Chen. A novel click model and its applications to online advertising. In *WSDM*, 2010. ACM Press. DOI: 10.1145/1718487.1718528. 6, 45, 46, 73, 83

Authors' Biographies

ALEKSANDR CHUKLIN

Aleksandr Chuklin is a Software Engineer working on search problems at Google Switzerland. Apart from his projects at Google he is also working with the Information and Language Processing Systems group at the University of Amsterdam on a number of research topics. He received his MSc degree from the Moscow Institute of Physics and Technology in 2012. His main research interests are modeling and understanding user behavior on a search engine result page. Aleksandr has a number of publications on click models and their applications at SIGIR, CIKM, ECIR. He is also PC member of the CIKM and WSDM conferences.

ILYA MARKOV

Ilya Markov is a postdoctoral researcher and SNF fellow at the University of Amsterdam. His research agenda builds around information retrieval methods for heterogeneous search environments. Ilya has experience in federated search, user behavior analysis, click models and effectiveness metrics. He is a PC member of leading IR conferences, such as SIGIR, WWW and ECIR, a PC chair of the RuSSIR 2015 summer school and a co-organizer of the IMine-2 task at NTCIR-12. Ilya is currently teaching an MSc course on web search and has previously taught information retrieval courses at the BSc and MSc levels and given tutorials at conferences and summer schools in IR (ECIR, RuS-SIR).

MAARTEN DE RIJKE

Maarten de Rijke is Professor of Computer Science at the University of Amsterdam. He leads a large team of researchers in information retrieval. His recent research focus is on (online) ranking and evaluation and on semantic search. Maarten has authored over 650 papers, many of which are core to this tutorial, and is Editor-in-Chief of *ACM Transactions on Information Systems*. He has supervised or is supervising over 40 Ph.D. students. He has taught at the primary school, high school, BSc, MSc and Ph.D. levels, as well as for general audiences, with recent tutorials at ECIR, ESSIR and SIGIR.

Index

Printed in the United States
by Baker & Taylor Publisher Services